Andy highlights and unpacks s
long-standing discipleship lesso
roots them into Jesus and skilfully applies them to our everyday lives. Relevant, practical and biblical teaching from an
experienced pastor – incredibly helpful for small groups or
individuals who want to grow as disciples of Jesus.

Revd Mark Madavan, pastor and speaker

After God's Heart is a book for every person who calls themselves a disciple of Christ. Through studying the life of King
David, Andy takes us along the well-trodden path of David's
triumphs and failures, encouraging us to think about our own
steps as we learn from his. While the stories may be familiar, the wisdom and truths that Andy pulls out are relevant,
challenging, inspiring and thought-provoking. This book is
appropriate for both individual and group study, giving theological as well as practical insights into navigating our everyday challenges with grace, wisdom and victory.

Jen Baker, author and speaker

In this book Andy faithfully explores the biblical life of David
in an accessible way which brings clarity and meaning with a
fresh approach. This book enables us to hold a mirror up to
our own leadership with insights into David's life and calling;
Andy draws you in to reflect on your leadership while being
vulnerable about his own journey.

After God's Heart draws the reader into self-reflection and
motivation to seek God in their own practices. This book is a
great resource for personal and group reflection.

Revd Hayley Young, Baptist regional minister,
president of the Baptist Union 2022–2023

It should be our surpassing ambition: to be women and men after God's own heart. In this lively, practical and readable book, Andy brings new life to a very old story, sharing life lessons that are vital for us all today. Highly recommended.

Jeff Lucas, author, speaker, broadcaster

Many of us will be familiar with the story of King David, one of the towering figures of the Old Testament. In this, his fourth book, Andy draws life lessons for us from a fresh look at David's story. Topics include God's unlikely choices, facing our giants, worship, and preparing for death, with helpful questions for reflection. As we look again at David's life, we are encouraged to draw closer to the God who, as Andy says in the first chapter, always sees us through his heart of grace.

Jeannie Kendall, author of Finding Our Voice *and* Held in Your Bottle

With this book, Andy presents a personable and vulnerable journey into the life of David. He explores the different aspects of David's life and the many ways we can learn from him about the nature of God. With thought-provoking questions and personal stories throughout, I found this book to offer a faithful companion to my own reflections on the Lord. There is so much to learn about the upside-down kingdom, and this book is a humble, honest and welcome contribution to that learning.

Lucy Grimble, songwriter and worship leader

After God's Heart

Life Lessons from King David

Andy Percey

Authentic

First published 2023 by Authentic Media Limited,
PO Box 6326, Bletchley, Milton Keynes, MK1 9GG.
authenticmedia.co.uk

British Library Cataloguing in Publication Data
A catalogue record for this book is available from the British Library.
ISBN: 978-1-78893-284-4
978-1-78893-285-1 (e-book)

Cover design by Vivian Hansen de los Rios
Printed and bound by Micropress Printers Ltd, Southwold, IP18 6SZ

For my Nana, Sheila

A woman after God's heart, whose example and wisdom continues to be a blessing in my and my family's life. I love you and am forever thankful for you.

Contents

Foreword

On holiday on Orkney a few years ago, I found myself discussing rock climbing with my host. He was telling me about people climbing the impressive 450-foot sea stack, 'The Old Man of Hoy'. 'Has anyone ever fallen off?' I asked. 'Ah no,' he said, 'but it's only a matter of time.'

Andy asked me to write the foreword to his new book because he found inspiration in a book I wrote over a decade ago now, *Barefoot Disciple*. That book begins with a fall. Not from The Old Man of Hoy, thank goodness, but down a staircase in the huge Victorian vicarage (huge enough to have two staircases) where I then lived. The reason for the fall was that I thought I could navigate my own home in the dark. The shock that I had stepped onto the top of the staircase rather than into the bathroom at two o'clock in the morning was a very rude, abrupt and dangerous awakening.

I hoped by writing about my tumble that my readers would put two and two together and reference the idea of the fall as the beginning of the Christian story, but I suspect that many just thought the writer was a fool. And a lucky one to have walked away with no more than a few bruises.

The story of the fall in Genesis is full of mystery, but whatever the details might mean it tells us that there is something deeply difficult for human beings when it comes to relating to God on God's terms. If it were possible for us to analyse ourselves, understand the problem of our relentless unholiness and put it right, then we could surely come up with a nice, simple procedure for living a good Christian life. Once that was cracked, we would sit down and, in a conflict-free meeting, design the kingdom of God. We would then build it without delay and in due course walk through the pearly gates with huge smiles on our faces.

The reality is very different. The gap between us and God, between our will and God's will, between our desires and God's intentions, is always there. That rift was healed by the sacrificial work of Christ's passion, death and resurrection, but even though we trust in our salvation we still find things going wrong in our lives. We make mistakes. We let ourselves down. We misunderstand. We fall – again, and again.

It's only a matter of time.

This is why we need wise guides and good companions on the journey of life. People who are wise not only in knowing what the right thing to do is, but who are good enough to be able to help us when we have been unwise, or worse. People who will meet us with sympathy when we are in a heap at the bottom of the stairs.

I have never met Andy, but what I have read in this book gives me the strong sense that he must be a wise guide and good companion – a real pastor. He shares his struggles with us. More than once he brings us close to the edge of life. And he makes us feel that if we were to open up to him we would find not judgement but patience and care. There is evident humility in these pages, and that's a much-needed and terribly underrated value and virtue today – in the church as much as everywhere else.

And so Andy's book isn't about Andy. It's about David – the uber-celebrity of the Hebrew people. David is the most vivid and iconic individual in the Old Testament, but he is no stained-glass window saint. Nor is he someone not to follow. But he is someone to learn from. Who else lived such a varied life? Who else expressed so many emotions so deeply? Who else was such a terrible sinner? Who else penned such songs of lament? Who else praised God with such fervour and abandon?

One of the things I really like about Andy's approach is that, like the Lord who selects David from among his brothers to be the future king, he looks not at the superficial matters but on, or perhaps rather into, the *heart*.

Why does he do this? It's because we come close to God not by considering great historical events or by analysing doctrines. We find ourselves becoming more attuned to God not by pontificating on the morals of others or by admiring people of unimpeachable virtue. We come close to God by imaginatively and prayerfully entering the inner dynamics of those who struggle to live faithfully, and seek, often despite themselves, to grow into the grace and truth that are fully revealed in Jesus Christ.

Stephen Cherry

Thanks

Whenever I sit down to write a book it can feel like a very isolated experience, just me and my laptop. As the process moves forward, more people are drawn in: other writers, speakers, family and friends. By the time this book arrives in your hands, there are lots of people to thank.

The wonderful team at Authentic, but specifically Claire for all your support in making this a better book. It's been a difficult few years for publishers, and I'm thankful for all the assistance and encouragement you have given me as a team along the way.

Gavin, Ros and Ian, for your wisdom and honesty, which have made this a more accessible book.

To my beautiful wife Bex. Thank you for supporting me when, after saying I was going to take a break from writing, just a few short weeks later I submitted a proposal for this book. Thank you for all you have shared on the journey to make this possible, during the difficult days when I found writing really hard, and the easier days. For all your wisdom and grace in bringing out the best in what I wanted to say, and your skill in helping me say it in the best way I could. Thank you for being you, and sharing the joyous adventure of life with me. I love you.

To our son Leo. Talking with you about David has made this book come alive for me in a special way, and I have treasured those precious chats. I pray that you might grow in the adventures of the great women and men of faith who came before us, shape your own adventures so others can learn from you, and keep growing as a man after God's heart. I love you.

Andy Percey
Summer 2022

Introduction

Ever since I was a boy I have loved stories of kings and knights, giants and quests. There was something about the adventure, the struggle, and the concept of 'the King' which captivated me.

As I grew up I discovered a deep love of history, fascinated by the kings and queens that have shaped the destiny of the United Kingdom, and the adventures and struggles they faced.

So often, though, it seems as if these adventures and struggles are from a different time, or relegated to the level of fables or fairy tales. After all, who has to fight a giant nowadays?

I have always loved the story of David in the Old Testament. Here is a boy taken from complete obscurity, even within his own family. This boy is anointed king in a hidden ceremony with the witnesses sworn to secrecy.

As a young man he has a noble yet unvalued job, and on a trip to the front lines of a war, he slays a giant.

He is a songwriter whose music both calms the troubled king of Israel and enrages him, leading to bouts of life-threatening violence.

David is forced to wait for his throne – to the point where he begins to wonder if what was promised will ever come to pass.

Finally he becomes king. The journey is just beginning.

He has to deal with choices that are meant to keep everyone happy but risk offending everyone. He has to deal with power and position and not let it get to his head, or trip over his own ego.

There is lust, murder and scandal to rival any political scandal of our times.

And he faces giants for a second time.

A lot is written about David in the Bible. In fact, the Bible devotes more text to David than to anyone else, apart from Jesus himself. His life is a significant one in the Scriptures, and so it's a life that is worth paying attention to.

David's story is one that captivates the imagination, and yet as we look more closely, we find it is a story that draws us in too – because the challenges that David faced are challenges that we also face. The time is different, the place is different, but the issues we face and the heart we are trying to develop and nurture underneath it all is the same.

The Bible makes a bold claim of David – that he was a man after God's own heart.[1]

Perhaps we have a lot to learn from David as we too seek to be people after God's heart.

I have been a local church pastor for over a decade, and having come across and walked with many different people, I am convinced that we are all trying to figure out, both as individuals and faith communities, what it means to follow Jesus today.

There are big challenges for us. The role and influence of the church within western society is shifting, and with it the model in which we have so often expressed our faith. But the call to discipleship is as important now as it has ever been.

One of the most influential books I have read is Stephen Cherry's *Barefoot Disciple*. In this book, Stephen tells us that the humble walk of discipleship is about learning. After all, the word 'disciple' comes from the Greek word for pupil or student. It is not, however, about information, but about transformation in the everyday moments of our lives. As Stephen reminds us: 'Discipleship involves learning in a way that is so everyday and ordinary that it is easily overlooked.'[2]

This is the walk that, as Christians, we have all been walking, each of us down the centuries. It is this constant march of the everyday disciple, of transformation birthed in a hundred different daily moments, that draws us into the flow of God's great and mighty cosmic rebirth.

It is a journey of spirituality which is rooted in the reality and earthiness of our lives. Jewish writer David Wolpe says: 'David's is a story not only of spirit but of blood and bone and flesh.'[3] Yes, there is a spiritual flow to the lessons we can learn from David's life, but these lessons appeal to us, and reach out to us, because they are formed in the flesh and bone of our real lives. We can see so much of ourselves in David.

It might feel at times as though this is a road we walk alone, but it is a road we all share. We are all walking one another home, because the path of discipleship, while at times lonely, is not designed to be taken alone. We have companions on the journey who walk alongside us and encourage us to keep going when we find it hard. They can model to us what this beautiful transformation looks like, and they can also serve as a warning of what happens when we fail to embrace it.

Not only are we encouraged and companioned on the road of discipleship by those who share it with us now, but we are also encouraged and companioned by those who have walked the road ahead of us and have now come to its destination.

Hebrews 11 is a great chapter of faith. It is the roll call of those who have walked the road before us: Abraham, Moses, Rahab, Gideon, Barak, Samson, Jephthah, David and Samuel and the prophets. The writer tells us that they are those 'who through faith conquered kingdoms, administered justice, obtained promises, shut the mouths of lions, quenched raging fire, escaped the edge of the sword, won strength out of weakness, became mighty in war, put foreign armies to flight'.[4]

Not only are these heroes of the faith women and men we can look back on and be inspired by, but they are actively cheering us on as we walk the road today. As the writer of Hebrews inspiringly goes on to say: 'Therefore, since we are surrounded by so great a cloud of witnesses, let us also lay aside every weight and the sin that clings so closely, and let us run with perseverance the race that is set before us'.[5]

David was certainly a man who earned his place in that chapter of the heroes of the faith. He earned that place, not through the great and mighty deeds themselves but by the everyday choices he made and the transformations he experienced. Did he make mistakes? Yes, spectacular ones, but we can learn from those too, and even they led to greater transformation.

So often, it is in the day-to-day routines that discipleship is lived. In many ways the big gestures of faith seem easier, but to live faithfully day by day can be more of a challenge.

When Jesus came out of the waters of baptism, the voice of the Father rang down from heaven: 'This is my Son, whom I love; with him I am well pleased.'[6] Pleased with what? At that moment in time, Jesus had not performed any miracles that we have heard about. He hadn't revealed himself to the world as the Messiah. He had no followers. What was the Father pleased with? Perhaps it was his everyday faithfulness up to that moment. He had been a good son, a good brother, a good worker, a faithful worshipper; perhaps what the Father was pleased with was his *heart*. The heart that David also reflected. The heart that is forged in the everyday moments.

Transformation can come through lessons we learn on the road of discipleship, and for David these were the foundation on which he stood to achieve the great things we often remember him for.

As the writer of Hebrews assures us, David now is part of that great cloud of witnesses that encourage us, that cheer us on as we too walk the road. He has run and finished his race, but there are lessons he learned which we can benefit from, leading us to greater transformation. As we learn these life lessons from a king, I pray that we might be unburdened more and more from the things that weigh us down, so that we might run the race that is set before us on the road of everyday discipleship, following after the one who is the only true King: the pioneer and perfecter of our faith, King Jesus.

Additional note from author

On 8 September 2022 Queen Elizabeth II died in Balmoral, Scotland. Her death brought to an end the longest reign of any British monarch, a reign that spanned seventy years. Whenever I lead a funeral I am struck by the challenge of how you 'sum up' a life, but in the days that followed the death of the Queen, commentators, writers and presenters had the immense challenge of doing just that.

One of the main themes that kept coming to the surface of the conversation was her faith and her example. The Queen had a living faith, one which provided the bedrock for her life both personally and in her role as Head of State. She spoke about it many times, but perhaps most poignantly during her Christmas messages to the nation.

Her example of a life dedicated to service is one that many have encouraged us to follow.

Queen Elizabeth was human; she made mistakes as well as achieving many great things. This is important to acknowledge when reflecting on a life, especially one that has been well lived. For both Queen Elizabeth II and King David, there are lessons we can learn as we reflect; not simply to emulate them in doing what they did, or avoiding what they failed to, but in looking to what gave their lives meaning and purpose. Both were monarchs who inherited great power and wealth, but who managed to avoid chasing after it because their eyes were fixed on something, or rather *someone*, else. At the Queen's funeral, the Archbishop of Canterbury said:

> 'Her Late Majesty's example was not set through her position or her ambition, but through who she followed . . . In all cases those who serve will be loved and remembered when those who cling to power and privileges are long forgotten.'[7]

As we reflect and remember, let us learn the lessons of a life well lived, and fix our eye once more on the one before whom all earthly rulers lay their crowns – King Jesus.

1

The Secret Anointing

Many of us will know of David the king, or David the song-writer, or David the giant-slayer; but when David burst on to the biblical scene it was in much more humble circumstances than those famous days to come.

The Obvious Choice?

When we compare how David was chosen to be king with the choosing of Israel's first king, Saul, we see that the two situations couldn't be more different.

In 1 Samuel 9 we read a description of Saul: 'There was not a man among the people of Israel more handsome than he; he stood head and shoulders above everyone else.'[1]

When people were choosing a king in the days of Saul and David, it wasn't about how well he dressed or how much money he had; he had to physically look the part. He had to be tall and strong, so that he could carry heavy weapons into battle and have the power to defeat the nation's enemies in times of war. This was how the kingdom would prosper.

This is why the leaders of many countries, to this day, display the might of their military by holding huge parades where their tanks and vehicle-mounted missiles are driven through the streets in front of cheering crowds, as the armies march behind and aircraft fly overhead – because it is in your ability to project strength that your security lies.

In this regard, Saul ticked all the boxes. He was physically fit, he was handsome, he looked like a king. He projected strength. He was the obvious choice.

What about David? We read the account of how David was chosen to be king, just seven chapters after Saul, in 1 Samuel 16:

The LORD said to Samuel, 'How long will you grieve over Saul? I have rejected him from being king over Israel. Fill your horn with oil and set out; I will send you to Jesse the Bethlehemite, for I have provided for myself a king among his sons.' Samuel said, 'How can I go? If Saul hears of it, he will kill me.' And the LORD said, 'Take a heifer with you, and say, "I have come to sacrifice to the LORD." Invite Jesse to the sacrifice, and I will show you what you shall do; and you shall anoint for me the one whom I name to you.' Samuel did what the LORD commanded, and came to Bethlehem. The elders of the city came to meet him trembling, and said, 'Do you come peaceably?' He said, 'Peaceably; I have come to sacrifice to the LORD; sanctify yourselves and come with me to the sacrifice.' And he sanctified Jesse and his sons and invited them to the sacrifice.

When they came, he looked on Eliab and thought, 'Surely the LORD's anointed is now before the LORD.' But the LORD said to Samuel, 'Do not look on his appearance or on the height of his stature, because I have rejected him; for the LORD does not see as mortals see; they look on the outward appearance, but the LORD looks on the heart.' Then Jesse called Abinadab, and made him pass before Samuel. He said, 'Neither has the LORD chosen this one.' Then Jesse made Shammah pass by. And he said, 'Neither has the LORD chosen this one.' Jesse made seven of his sons pass before Samuel, and Samuel said to Jesse, 'The LORD has not chosen any of these.' Samuel said to Jesse, 'Are all your sons here?' And he said, 'There remains yet the youngest, but he is keeping the sheep.' And Samuel said to Jesse, 'Send and bring him; for we will not sit down until he comes here.' He sent and brought him in. Now he was ruddy, and had beautiful eyes, and was handsome. The LORD said, 'Rise and anoint him; for this is the one.' Then Samuel took the horn of oil, and anointed him in the presence of his brothers; and the spirit of the LORD came mightily upon David from that day forward. Samuel then set out and went to Ramah.[2]

What is interesting in this account of how David is chosen to be king is that right at the start, David isn't even there. He is so unlikely a choice that the family don't even send for him when Samuel arrives. He is out in the fields looking after the sheep, and the other seven sons of Jesse are brought to meet the prophet. Why? Because they look the part. They, like Saul, fit the bill – the idea that in order to prosper you have to project strength.

See in verse 6 how similar the oldest brother Eliab is to what we have already read about Saul. Samuel is even taken in by this man-mountain, and thinks, *Ah yes, the Lord's anointed.* But God speaks words of correction to the prophet, warning him not to look at the outward appearance or the physical stature of the man. This was going to be a very different choice and a different way of choosing. This was not about the projection of the power and strength of a king; God had other plans in mind.

This was a rejection of the dominant world system. The people of Israel had asked God for a king to rule over them and to keep them safe. That system, though, was always flawed because the people would rely on it instead of on God. It was never going to end well, and in the end, with Saul, it didn't. Here, God was choosing a king who would point people to himself. This was in some ways 'regime change', but it was also culture change, and that is always very threatening to the interest groups that hold the power in a society. We see this in the clandestine way in which the choosing of David takes place. Samuel is genuinely in fear of his life because he knows how Saul will react if he finds out what is happening.

It is a common reaction. We see it in the New Testament in the response of Herod to the news that the magi have come searching for a new king. We see it in our modern world. As I write this, the 2020 US election has just taken place with the Democratic presidential challenger Joe Biden projected to oust the Republican incumbent Donald Trump. The reaction of Donald Trump is the same as the reaction Samuel fears from Saul: those in power, whose desire is to retain the projection of power and strength and prosperity, will do whatever it takes to hold on to that power.

That is the system that needs to change, and that is partly what we see going on here with the choosing of David. It is the rejecting of the old system, and the bringing in of something new.

What about the dominant system in our world today? We don't have the same focus on physical power and strength as our ancestors had in the ancient world. Our world today is based on an economic system, but the principles of this system remain the same. It is still about the projection of strength and power. We live in a world where the rich prosper and the poor suffer, where the system is tilted in favour of those who maintain it, not those who are failed by it. In the days of ancient Sparta, children born with physical disabilities were left outside the city walls to die of exposure, because the system of the day was about physical strength and it couldn't carry the weakness of anyone who didn't prop that system up.

Today, those who are economically weak – the poor – are left to die on the streets of our cities because the system cannot carry their 'weakness'.

Of course there have to be conversations about how best to help people, and there will always be some who are seen to be abusing the system of support and help; but let's not fool ourselves into believing that the dominant system of our twenty-first-century world is tilted in favour of the poor.

Why focus on these systems? Because these dominant systems also exist within our church culture and directly affect how we see our calling as Christians.

I have heard so many people in church over the years expressing the view that they have nothing to offer because they can't give financially as much as others, or they don't measure up to 'the people up the front' – the leadership team. They feel as though there is a type of person whom God can call, and unless you fit that mould, unless you are a person who fits the system (and yes, there are systems within church life too), then you can't be used by God.

I have met so many gifted, passionate people who could offer so much to the world just by being themselves, just by living true to the man or woman God has made them to be, just by singing their song, who feel that they just can't do that because they don't measure up to some standard of worthiness that they believe is required in order for God to use them.

As churches, we are failing those people in the same way that our culture fails those who die on our streets, and in the same way that the ancient Spartans failed those who were left outdoors to die of exposure. Why? Because we are giving them the message that you have to be a certain type of person to be of use, and – even more worryingly – that you have to be a certain type of person to be valued! When we do that, what we portray are the views that are perpetuated by the dominant power systems of the world, and they have no place within the church.

Having seen how the old system works in the story of David – the physicality, strength and dominance of the powerful – we now see how David stands in contrast.

This was a party David wasn't even invited to. That is significant because right from the very start David stands apart from this rejected system. He doesn't fit into it. He is the youngest son. In fact, the word that is used in the biblical text to describe his youth implies insignificance.[3] According to Hebrew scholar Robert Alter, David is a 'kind of male Cinderella left to his domestic chores instead of being invited to the party'.[4]

In fact, when we are first introduced to this youngest son of Jesse, we are not even told his name. His father simply says: 'There remains yet the youngest, but he is keeping the sheep.'[5] On the half a dozen occasions in this short passage where David could have been mentioned by name, he isn't. It is only at the very end of the passage that we learn David's name.

Again, this highlights the fact that something different is happening here. Even when Samuel anoints him, David isn't mentioned by name. This happens only when he is anointed by the Holy Spirit.

David's identity doesn't come in the anointing with oil for the position of kingship. His identity comes in the anointing of the Holy Spirit to be the person that God has called him to be.

Comparing Ourselves to Others

One of the challenges we find when we feel as though we don't measure up is that we can spend endless time comparing ourselves to others. Not all comparison is bad, as we will go on to see in our next chapter, but the sort of comparison that leaves you feeling woefully inadequate and with a diminished sense of self-worth and value is never good.

The problem is that this is rife in our society!

If we look at social media today, we see immediately that there is so much negative comparison that takes place. A large part of people's sense of value comes from the response they get online to things that they post. It might involve trying to get that perfect picture that measures up to the 'ideal family' shots that you see on other people's profiles. Or checking the number of likes or comments a post gets compared to others. As a church leader, during the recent period of online church, it might be comparing numbers of people logging on to other churches, or comparing your current numbers to those earlier on in the Covid-19 pandemic when engagement was higher.

The challenge with this kind of comparison is that we will always come off second best. Why? Because no matter how many likes you have, no matter how many comments you get, no matter how 'perfect' that picture you take is, there will always be someone who has more likes, or who takes a more ideal picture. The problem is not 'out there'; the problem is within us. That sense of validation comes from others because so often our ego is fuelled by the comparisons we make with others.

We become the sidekicks of our own lives because we are always looking for heroes 'out there' somewhere. We end up not being the 'obvious choice' in our own lives. Perhaps one of the bravest things we can do is to stop looking out there and start to look inwards, and as the song says, to 'search for the hero inside'. It might not be what we expected. It might not measure up to anyone else's standards. But really, what other people think of us is none of our business.

So was David the obvious choice to be king? By any of the standards of his day, no, he was not the obvious choice. What about by God's standards? Clearly he was! God is the God who uses the weak ones to shame the strong, and chooses the foolish to shame the wise.[6]

It was God who reminded his people, when he made a covenant with them at Sinai, to not fall into the trap of thinking that their prosperity and successes came from their own power and strength:

> Take care that you do not forget the LORD your God, by failing to keep his commandments, his ordinances, and his statutes, which I am commanding you today. When you have eaten your fill and have built fine houses and live in them, and when your herds and

flocks have multiplied, and your silver and gold is multiplied, and all that you have is multiplied, then do not exalt yourself, forgetting the LORD your God, who brought you out of the land of Egypt, out of the house of slavery, who led you through the great and terrible wilderness, an arid waste-land with poisonous snakes and scorpions. He made water flow for you from flint rock, and fed you in the wilderness with manna that your ancestors did not know, to humble you and to test you, and in the end to do you good. Do not say to yourself, 'My power and the might of my own hand have gained me this wealth.' But remember the LORD your God, for it is he who gives you power to get wealth, so that he may confirm his covenant that he swore to your ancestors, as he is doing today.[7]

And it was God who spoke through the prophet Zechariah, speaking truth to power: '"Not by might nor by power, but by my Spirit," says the LORD Almighty.'[8]

When measured against these standards, David was the obvious choice – a young man whose strength and identity came, not through physical attributes or position or the accolades of others, but through the anointing of the Spirit of God.

God's Obvious Choice Is Often the Least Obvious Choice

Shane Claiborne puts it beautifully well when he says: 'Yahweh continues to be careful to choose the weakest, most unlikely characters to be the heroes of the liberation story, lest we be tempted to think we did it ourselves, with our own power or might or ingenuity.'[9]

We see this with the calling of the disciples. The young men whom Jesus called were certainly not the best of the best, or the religious elite. We don't know what all of them did before Jesus called them, but for some we do have a bit of background. Andrew, Peter, James and John were fishermen:

> As [Jesus] walked by the Sea of Galilee, he saw two brothers, Simon, who is called Peter, and Andrew his brother, casting a net into the lake – for they were fishermen. And he said to them, 'Follow me, and I will make you fish for people.' Immediately they left their nets and followed him. As he went from there, he saw two other brothers, James son of Zebedee and his brother John, in the boat with their father Zebedee, mending their nets, and he called them. Immediately they left the boat and their father, and followed him.[10]

These were not well-educated men. They would have dropped out of formal education in the synagogue in order to work in the family business, and because they are working in the family business we know they are not following another rabbi. So we know, in terms of the intellectual and religious circles of their day, these men don't fit in. They are also not likely to be wealthy. While fishing was an important business, it was not a business that was going to make you rich.

We know that Matthew was a tax collector: 'As Jesus was walking along, he saw a man called Matthew sitting at the tax booth; and he said to him, "Follow me." And he got up and followed him.'[11]

To say that tax collectors were unpopular in the time of Jesus would be a massive understatement. They were responsible for collecting the tax that was to be paid by the Jewish people to Rome, the occupying power, and their association with the Roman oppressors meant they were often hated. If taking your money and giving it to the enemy wasn't bad enough, they often charged more than the tax itself and kept the money for themselves.

Unlike the fishermen, the tax collector would be wealthy, but by any political or religious circle of the day, Matthew would have been shunned.

The point here is that Jesus doesn't choose his disciples based on the religious, social, political or educational values of the day. He doesn't choose the brightest, or the richest, or the popular, or the most pious. He calls ordinary people to be part of his extraordinary ministry.

We see this throughout the Bible.

From Jacob who stole the birthright of his older brother, to Moses who murdered an Egyptian guard, from Tamar who pretended to be a prostitute to seduce her father-in-law, to Rahab who actually was a prostitute, the Bible is full of ordinary people – those who don't fit the mould, who don't measure up, who are not the obvious choices. These are the people God calls, because they are the ones who best display his glory. These are the people in whose weakness his strength can be made manifest, and in whose foolishness his wisdom can be displayed.

As Shane Claiborne reminds us: 'Some of us have been told our entire lives that we are wretched, but the gospel reminds us that we are beautiful.'[12]

It might be that you feel as though, in the life of your church, or faith community, or family, or workplace or social group, that you are the Cinderella not invited to the ball. It might be that you are happy about that because you feel as though you don't have anything to bring to the party anyway. You might not feel like an Eliab, or a Saul, and so you think, *What could God possibly need from a person like me?* According to Eugene Peterson, 'Election into God's purposes isn't by popular vote. Election into God's purposes isn't based on proven ability or potential promise.'[13]

What you bring is who you are. You are valuable, you have worth, you can make a difference, you can shine in the places you already are. The anointing with oil symbolizes stepping into a new role, such as becoming king, but it is the anointing of God's Spirit that empowers you to live for him within that role. This is a greater power; the anointing of the Spirit is greater than any 'anointing' you can receive through human recognition or accreditation.

As I move into my second decade of pastoral ministry, I know that there have been times when I felt as if I deserved to be where I was. I remember thinking, when I arrived at Bible college in 2006, that I had 'arrived'. I believe that the flaw in my character and mindset that gave birth to that view was exacerbated by a church culture of celebrity which values the people 'up the front', seeing them as somehow more deserving and worthy, or special, than those not at the front.

However, the more I entered into ministry, the more I became aware of just how painfully I didn't measure up. Along the way I made mistakes, I hurt people, and I realized very clearly that whatever position I held, the one constant was me. The baggage that I carried, the ways in which I fell short, the issues I faced were still there. If ministry was about what I had to offer, then I was becoming increasingly aware that I had very little to offer other than my brokenness. I remember a period when I had to take some time out for health reasons, and during this period my family and I attended another church in the area. For me, worship became a time when I wept through all the songs and then went to the front after the service to be prayed for. It was the same week after week – tears and support. It was painful, but it was healing – because the real healing that needed to happen was to my heart, and unless that changed, unless that healed, then no other healing was going to take place.

What was so important during that time, and why I treasure those services so much today, was that my worship was real. When everything is stripped away and we come to God as we are, with no mask or pretence, there is a purity, a beauty. Not that I was beautiful – far from it – but having felt that for years I had to wear a mask, to have it removed meant freedom.

What I came to understand was that when your heart is healed, any other qualification doesn't matter; the only qualification is a heart that God has transformed and is causing to beat in time with his. The only thing that matters is that we have prayed, as David prays in the Psalms: 'Create in me a clean heart, O God . . .'[14] Some get that transplant with ease, while others have to wait until their own heart has failed.

However we come, what we all have in common is that it is no longer our own behaviour or ability or righteousness that qualifies us, but the transforming power of God's Spirit and the renewing of our hearts through his love and grace. No dominant system in the world, past, present or future, can bring about that change, and ultimately that is why they fail – because they cannot bring about in each and every human soul what is needed. Not the anointing of the head for position, but the anointing of the heart for transformation. It is that transformation that all of creation is desperate for, and which every human soul craves. We crawl across the desert to find it, to drink from it – only for some of us to get stuck in the desert drinking sand. All we need to do is call out for it, lift our eyes and open our hearts, and be refreshed.

The Lord Sees with the Heart

Having seen how the people God chooses are not always the obvious choices based on the values of the world – and that was certainly the case for David at the start of his story – we now come to look at a key verse in this opening narrative: 'But the LORD said to Samuel, "Do not look on his appearance or on the height of his stature, because I have rejected him; for the LORD does not see as mortals see; they look on the outward appearance, but the LORD looks on the heart."'[15]

Now the Bible version that I have quoted above is fairly standard in the way it structures this text, and it leads to the traditional interpretation of the verse, which is that people look at the outward appearance but God looks at the heart.

As human beings, we often judge by what we see, and we tend to judge by outward appearance. It might not be the most lasting impression, but it is usually the way we see in the immediate moment.

For example, in the church where I am the pastor, in the centre of the city of Bath, we house the city's homeless shelter which is run by Julian House. Usually that means there are a lot of homeless people who congregate on the steps of our church building. I know that there are some individuals in the church who struggle with how this 'looks', and they are not alone. I have met some in the city leadership over the years (thankfully a minority) who have expressed the view that the main part of the problem is how this 'looks', and that it tarnishes the image of Bath, especially for tourists. It is not a view I share, but it is an example of how easy it is to focus on the appearance of things and not look more deeply.

When I first came to preach at this church in 2014, I asked whether it would be helpful to come dressed especially smartly. I was told, 'Come dressed in what you are comfortable in.' So I did! I wore what I normally wore when I led services in the church where I was pastor at the time, which was jeans and a shirt (not tucked in!). Many in the congregation at the church in Bath are older folk, more traditional and more formal. So my style was not something that went unnoticed. In fact, someone in the church when they were discussing my visit actually quoted 1 Samuel 16:7! I dress a little smarter now, so that what I'm saying and what I'm doing are not lost because of what I'm wearing.

It is very easy to focus on appearance.

We are told that we shouldn't judge a book by its cover, but if you are anything like me then you will overlook a book if you don't like its cover, never actually picking it up. What's on the cover is important to us.

The implication for our traditional interpretation of 1 Samuel 16:7 is that God looks much more deeply. God opens the book to look inside. God cares very much about what is going on in our hearts, about who we are, not simply how we appear.

However, there is another way to read this verse. In his Bible translation with commentary, Robert Alter offers this rendering: 'For not as man sees does God see. For man sees with the eyes and the LORD sees with the heart.'[16]

This might seem quite similar to the version quoted above, but there is a depth in the subtle difference between these translations that is worth exploring. Our traditional translations say that God looks *at* the heart, but Alter's translation says that God looks *with* the heart.

As human beings we do not see with our eyes. We look with our eyes, but we actually see with the brain. Light in the world around us hits the retina at the back of the eye, and special cells there called photoreceptors (light receivers) take this light and turn it into electrical signals which then travel down the optic nerve into the brain, and the brain then turns these electrical signals into images. We look with the eyes, and we see with the brain. So when we look with our eyes, we aren't really seeing; we are just looking. We are acknowledging the presence of what is there right in front of us. And when we look in this way, a lot of information is missed out. The way we see isn't just based on the action of looking, because our brains discount information that isn't relevant to us. So, as I sit here in my study, my eyes will pick up lots of different things around me, through my peripheral vision and as I glance around, but my brain will say that this isn't relevant, so I won't 'see' it.

And what we do 'see', we see filtered through our experiences and judgements.

But this is not how God sees. God sees *with* the heart. In biblical philosophy the heart is often thought of as the seat of understanding and insight. So when God sees, he is doing so with both understanding and insight. He knows us. He understands us. He truly sees us:

> You have searched me, Lord,
>   and you know me.

You know when I sit and when I rise;
　　you perceive my thoughts from afar.
You discern my going out and my lying down;
　　you are familiar with all my ways.
Before a word is on my tongue
　　you, Lord, know it completely.
You hem me in behind and before,
　　and you lay your hand upon me.
Such knowledge is too wonderful for me,
　　too lofty for me to attain.[17]

When God looks with understanding and insight, God looks with the heart – the heart of who God is. And God's heart is looking for that which will reflect it back, to find something of God in the other, a point of connection and relationship. He wants to know that here is a heart that is like his heart.

So when God says of David, 'Here is a man after my own heart,' it certainly doesn't mean that all the choices David makes are like God's choices. Many of the choices David makes are inexcusable. As Max Lucado puts it: 'He stared down Goliath, yet ogled at Bathsheba; defied God-mockers in the valley, yet joined them in the wilderness . . . He could lead armies but he couldn't manage a family.'[18]

Despite the fact that David's heart swings one way and the other, when God says David is a man after his own heart, it means that God's heart looks at David and sees something of his own heart within him. That should give all of us who make mistakes, whose hearts are easily moved, a great deal of hope.

Our anointing isn't about measuring up to some religious standard. It isn't about what we do in church, whether we have prayed the right prayers or sung the right hymns, or ticked the boxes; whether we have served on the leadership team for the past 100 years; or whether we have a car parking space right next to the church.

God is looking at your heart today, with his heart, looking to see if there is a connection, a mirror back. And as God looks at my heart, and your heart, will he say, 'Ah yes, this heart is like mine'?

Whether or not we seem like the obvious choice, whether or not we feel like the heroes of our own stories, this is less important than having a heart that mirrors something of God's heart. God isn't seeking professional Christians, or Instagram Christians. God isn't even seeking heroes. God is seeking those who will, in the fragile beauty of our broken humanity, reflect something of who he is. He seeks people who will connect with him in the vulnerability of relationship.

In the little town of Bethlehem, David's town, many years later, there would come another king who was the unexpected choice. The one that people didn't want and didn't think they needed. He might not have been seen as the hero who would rescue the people from the problems they saw. But this young hero reflected God's heart perfectly, mirrored it exactly. Not in the expectations of the religious, or the might of the powerful, but in the fragile beauty and brokenness of a human heart, and in the vulnerability of relationship.

Will you stand with Jesus? Will you dare to live as the unexpected choice? Will you be heroic enough to step away from the dominant systems of our time, and stand in your anointing as the one who reflects something of the beautiful heart of God?

Questions for Reflection

1. Can you think of any other stories, from the Bible, fiction or real life, where 'the least obvious choice' is the hero? Why do we like these stories?

2. How is our society challenged by God's insistence on using the weakest to fulfil his purpose?

3. How can we work with God to challenge the systems we see around us?

4. What does comparing ourselves to others do to us?

5. How can we start seeing ourselves and others 'with the heart', as God does?

6. What does it mean to be a man or woman 'after God's heart'?

7. 'Some of us have been told our entire lives that we are wretched, but the gospel reminds us that we are beautiful.' How can you walk in this truth today, for yourself and others?

2

Facing Your Giant

Now the Philistines gathered their forces for war and assembled at Sokoh in Judah. They pitched camp at Ephes Dammim, between Sokoh and Azekah. Saul and the Israelites assembled and camped in the Valley of Elah and drew up their battle line to meet the Philistines. The Philistines occupied one hill and the Israelites another, with the valley between them.

A champion named Goliath, who was from Gath, came out of the Philistine camp. His height was six cubits and a span. He had a bronze helmet on his head and wore a coat of scale armour of bronze weighing five thousand shekels; on his legs he wore bronze greaves, and a bronze javelin was slung on his back. His spear shaft was like a weaver's rod, and its iron point weighed six hundred shekels. His shield bearer went ahead of him.

Goliath stood and shouted to the ranks of Israel, 'Why do you come out and line up for battle? Am I not a Philistine, and are you not the servants of Saul? Choose a man and let him come down to me. If he is able to fight and kill me, we will become your subjects; but if I overcome him and kill him, you will become our subjects and serve us.' Then the Philistine said, 'This day I defy the armies of Israel! Give me a man and let us fight each other.' On hearing the Philistine's words, Saul and all the Israelites were dismayed and terrified.[1]

One of the things that really strikes me about the Bible is that it is a story of ordinary women and men who are drawn into the purposes of an extraordinary God. The great heroes of our faith were people who understood the reality that life is at times very challenging, but that it is also full of beauty and joy. They were aware that the call to follow God – to be renewed and transformed into the people he has created us to be – is not easy, but it is the deepest blessing that we can know.

We too understand that both the good and the bad are realities of life. We know that God loves us, that God gives his best to us, and that God blesses us because he wants us to thrive, not just survive. But we also know that life at times can be hard, both physically in getting through the day and spiritually in pushing forward towards our goal of being transformed into the likeness of Jesus. David, like all the saints, had those times too. In this chapter we will see David face his first, perhaps 'biggest', and certainly most famous challenge: Goliath.

In the previous chapter we explored the moment when we are first introduced to David. This happens in a passive sense, in that David doesn't speak at all in the encounter with Samuel which leads to his anointing. We know who he is – his name, where he is from, his family – but we do not know him. This will change in the passage we are exploring in this chapter, when we hear David speak for the first time. Many biblical scholars highlight the importance of an individual's first words in Scripture for presenting to us something of the person themselves, something of their character. What is interesting with David is that we are presented with a bit of a mixed bag, as he asks: 'What will be done for the man who kills this Philistine and removes this disgrace from Israel?

Who is this uncircumcised Philistine that he should defy the armies of the living God?'[2]

In these words there is self-interest, which in many ways always sits in the background throughout David's story; he often wanted to know what might be in it for him. But there is also a sense of patriotism and zeal, which similarly defines David's character going forwards. This paradox, this contradiction, is significant in helping us to understand something of David's nature, because what we see here is both sides of the man. We know that David is a man after God's own heart, but as David Wolpe highlights in his book on David, it is a 'divided heart'.[3]

This is something that all of us can relate to, because we are complex people. Our actions and our motives aren't always as pure as we would want them to be, even if our hearts are in the right place. There is light and dark within all of us, but at times the real challenge is in that middle ground where it doesn't seem to be obviously light or dark, but murky. David too is a man whose story at times can be described as murky, a man with a divided heart, but a man who catches something of the divine heart at the same time.

These first words are significant and revealing, but as the story progresses they are almost eclipsed by this most famous of encounters.

What Are Your Giants?

If David thought that his life would continue as before – the quiet life of a shepherd boy – then he was about to find out differently: God's purpose was leading him out of obscurity and into the limelight.

There were lessons that David had learned in the fields, while keeping watch over his sheep, that would help him along the way.

As a shepherd he had found himself in tight spots on regular occasions. In 1 Samuel 17:34 we hear of David fighting off bears and lions to defend the sheep. He was no stranger to hard times, long nights awake and tiring days. His hardest challenge, though, in those early years, came in facing the giant Goliath.

I think we know, too, that in our own lives our hardest challenges come in facing our own giants – the things that stare us in the face unmoving, and call us out to what we believe to be certain failure when facing them.

The Israelites were at war with their most famous enemy, the Philistines, and were being terrorized by their champion Goliath.

We are told in the passage above, in 1 Samuel 17:4–7, that Goliath was a little hard to miss! He stood over 9 feet tall (2.75 metres) and wore gleaming metal armour weighing around 57 kilograms.

The giants we face in our own lives can be a little harder to spot. That's why we need to have a degree of self-awareness to know how to answer the question 'What are your giants?' Many people never ask themselves the question, perhaps because they are trying to keep themselves distracted as an avoidance tactic; or they live in a state of denial because they don't want to face reality, accept they have a weakness and admit they are not completely in control. But we all have giants. They might not look like Goliath, they might not live up a beanstalk and threaten to grind your bones to make their bread, but they are no less fierce and potentially no less deadly.

For some, the giant can be habitual sin, the thing that they just can't seem to shake. For others, it can be a deep inner battle over self-worth and value. For one person it may be debilitating grief, for another excruciating loneliness, for yet another a paralysing fear of failure and rejection. Maybe it's a loss of health and the consequences of how that plays out in your future. The list goes on and on, but whatever you perceive to be the giant or giants in your life, I believe the universally defining factor is that the giant calls you out and attempts to make you believe the opposite of what the voice of truth, the Holy Spirit of our living Lord, is telling you.

Whether it is sin, self-loathing, grief, loneliness (fill in the appropriate blank), the Lord has something freeing and gracious, affirming and challenging to say to you, and the giant is desperate to try and outshout God's voice of truth.

We see this with the taunts of Goliath throughout 1 Samuel 17, trying to drown out the shouts of David, who comes in the name of the Lord so that Israel may no longer live in fear. Do you see a pattern here with your own giants?

When the Lord says to you regarding your sin, 'I have come to set you free, and my grace is sufficient for you,' the giant says, 'But you've done this so many times already.'

When the Lord says regarding self-loathing, 'I value you – you are precious in my sight,' the giant says, 'Maybe *now*, but like all those others, won't he just let you down and cut you off?'

When the Lord says regarding grief, 'I have come to bind up the broken-hearted – let me walk with you in this valley,' the giant says, 'It's too hard, it hurts too much, and how could he have let this happen anyway?'

When the Lord says regarding loneliness, 'I am with you, even until the end of time,' the giant says, 'Where was he when . . .'

The giant always shouts the opposite to the Lord's voice of truth.

What are your giants? The reason I ask is so that, as we move on and look a little more closely at how to face them, you can have in your mind your own giant. I want us to be able to apply God's truth specifically and strategically as we go through this chapter because, in the same way that David's future as a man after God's heart was dependent on him surviving and defeating Goliath, so I believe that if we are to be a people after God's own heart, if we are to walk in the anointing and calling of God into the future God has for us, we need to know how God empowers us to face our own giants.

How Do We Face Our Giants?

David had a very clear strategy when it came to facing Goliath:

> David said to the Philistine, 'You come against me with sword and spear and javelin, but I come against you in the name of the LORD Almighty, the God of the armies of Israel, whom you have defied. This day the LORD will deliver you into my hands, and I'll strike you down and cut off your head. This very day I will give the carcasses of the Philistine army to the birds and the wild animals, and the whole world will know that there is a God in Israel. All those gathered here will know that it is not by sword or spear that the LORD saves; for the battle is the LORD's, and he will give all of you into our hands.'[4]

Something more than physical strength would be needed to win this battle, and David was under no illusion. Nothing else but the Lord's strength would see the battle won and the giant defeated.

But how do we fight? How do we come face to face with our giants . . . come face to face with those mountains . . . come face to face with the Goliaths in our life, and not just attempt to sweep them under the carpet but to move on from them, get past them, and when it comes right down to it, defeat them?

There are a couple of things that David did when facing his giant, strategies that he used, which you and I can use as well as we stand face to face with our own giants. Do you still have your giant in your head? Keep it in mind as we look at what David did in 1 Samuel 17.

1. David faced up to his giant

A critical thing to do with those giants in our lives is actually to face them. There are times in life when we are at heightened levels of emotion, and it is often only then that those fearful things come to the surface. And when they do, we never fully speak about them, because often we don't want to face them or bring them into the light. But how important that is if we are to defeat our giants!

I am aware that there is split opinion on the *Harry Potter* books, but I know that many Christians have read them. There are similarities between these books and the story of David and Goliath. Harry Potter has an enemy in the story, and that enemy is Voldemort. But nobody will say Voldemort's name. Only Harry Potter will do that.

Speak to any psychologist and they will tell you that when you name something, when you face up to something, you can begin to get a handle on it, and when you do, half the battle is won. In our church we have several Alcoholics Anonymous (AA) groups that meet every day of the week, as well as other support groups for gambling, narcotics and sex addiction. When you join such a group, one of the key elements is to admit that you have a problem. Why else would you be there? The truth is that admitting you have a problem and seeking help and support to overcome it is perhaps the bravest thing you can do. The world may look at the members of these groups and pity them as people who have 'got a lot of problems', but in reality these are the people who are learning how to overcome their problems and face their giants. Don't pity them; learn from them.

David is sent to the camp of the Israelite army to find out how his brothers are doing. Anyone who has had a child serve in the armed forces, or in a combat zone, or in a dangerous profession will know the worry that Jesse felt. So he sends David, who has once again been kept behind. Just as we saw in the previous chapter, where David was so unlikely to be the choice for king that he wasn't even asked to leave the fields, so in this chapter David is so unlikely to be the warrior that he is kept at home. He is not, in the eyes of his family or his society, a fighter.

When he arrives to find out how his brothers are, and how the army are, he discovers that in many ways they are fine. They are camped on one side of the valley, and the Philistines are camped on the other side of the valley. There is no fighting, no bloodshed; everything seems OK.

That's the key word: *seems*. It seems OK because all that's happening is Goliath shouting out taunts against the Israelites and their God. Sticks and stones, right?

But the problem is that those words, and the presence of the giant, have brought fear into the camp. The Israelite soldiers are not stationary because of confidence or for strategic purposes; they are paralysed by fear: 'On hearing the Philistine's words, Saul and all the Israelites were dismayed and terrified.'[5] That's the reaction of the warriors in the camp. Even the king, who we are told was the tallest man in Israel, was quaking in his boots at the sight of this giant.

In one sense it does not matter how strong you think you are, or how impressive the string of victories you have amassed; when it comes to the giant, even the biggest and the bravest of us can be left camped on the other side of the valley, paralysed by fear.

It takes the little shepherd boy, the one who was left at home, to teach his big brothers, all the king's army and all the king's men that the only way to move out of fear was to face the giant in God's strength.

Ian Coffey reminds us that 'when we face "giants" we need to resist the longing to run away. The determination to face an issue is step one on the road to winning.'[6]

Face your giant. As David says: 'Who is this Philistine who defies the armies of the living God?'[7] All of a sudden, that giant doesn't look so big after all. This is a massive thing for us to do as we seek to battle our giants, just as David did.

2. David turned his back on the discouragers

I'm the oldest of my siblings, and I can tell you that David's brothers spoke to him as only older children can do to their younger siblings; older siblings have a habit of thinking they know best.

In life there are all kinds of people who will do the same. I wonder if you have experienced that? In my own life, and even in ministry, I have experienced it. I'm not talking about those people who need to tell us hard things from time to time in order to help us grow. We need those people in our lives and in our congregations. As it says in Proverbs:

> As iron sharpens iron,
>> so one person sharpens another.[8]

The important thing to note in this verse is that the purpose is to sharpen. There are those who bang against you, and their purpose is to blunt you, or even if that is not their purpose, you come away feeling battered and blunted. There are also those rare and treasured friends who will bang against you in order to sharpen you. We need wisdom to discern who those precious and trusted people are.

I remember hearing a prayer once that has stuck with me over the years: 'Lord, may those who love us, love us. And those who don't love us, Lord, please turn their hearts. And if not their hearts, Lord, turn their ankles, so that we may know them by their limping. Amen.' If God were to really answer this prayer, I wonder how many people in your life would be limping? How many people in your church would be limping?

There are certainly people around us, in every sphere of life, who often say, 'You can't do this. You can't do that.' Or: 'It just can't be done!'

The American politician Robert Kennedy is once reported to have said that 'one fifth of the people are against everything all the time'.

So the question we need to ask ourselves is whether those people are for us. Are they saying things to sharpen us, to help us to grow, to encourage us and take us deeper with God? Or are they trying to discourage us, to knock us down in order to boost their own ego at our expense?

One of the things I have had to learn – and sometimes the hard way in over a decade of pastoral ministry – is that you have to be careful who you listen to. This is especially important when there are discouragers around. Just like the voices of the giants we face, these negative voices can distract us from hearing God's voice of truth. But when we listen to that voice, when we choose to listen to the life-giving and grace-filled voice of God, then we can do far more than we think we can.

3. David created comparisons

> David said to Saul, 'Your servant has been keeping his father's sheep. When a lion or a bear came and carried off a sheep from the flock, I went after it, struck it and rescued the sheep from its mouth. When it turned on me, I seized it by its hair, struck it and killed it. Your servant has killed both the lion and the bear; this uncircumcised Philistine will be like one of them, because he has defied the armies of the living God. The LORD who rescued me from the paw of the lion and the paw of the bear will rescue me from the hand of this Philistine.'[9]

David came across a unique situation when facing Goliath, but what he did was to look back and make comparisons with things he had done before, to help him when facing his present danger. 'I killed lions. I protected my sheep. I've dealt with the bears. It's not quite like Goliath, but it's close enough to let me know that I can do it again.' And *our* past victories are close enough for us to know that we can do it again as well.

During the recent global pandemic, many have had to face giants. Giants of loneliness and isolation. In the UK, people had to face these giants throughout the first lockdown from March 2020, and the second lockdown in November 2020. At the time of writing, they are having to face them again through the third lockdown of January 2021. Part of my encouragement to them, and to the church, is to remind them that we have made it through the previous ones, and so we know that we can make it through this one as well. By creating that comparison, we can draw strength to help us with the giants that we face today.

The same is true when it comes to facing milestones around bereavement. When it comes to Christmas, or birthdays, or anniversaries, we tend to think a little more about the loved ones we have lost, and we can feel their absence more keenly. But we know, no matter how hard it is, that we can make it through those tough times because we have made it through before.

David knew that he could face his giant because it was God who had taken him this far and he would take him all the way. And if we trust the Lord, who has seen us through in the past, to help us with the giants we face now, then we will see this through as well.

We can also be encouraged by looking at how others have dealt with their giants. I heard a story once from the Second World War of a soldier who was in a prisoner-of-war camp and was placed in solitary confinement as punishment for trying to escape. He had been kept in a box-like crate for two weeks, and he said he couldn't take it any more. He began to mumble and groan, as I know I would have done, and then he began to hear somebody next to him speaking to him.

It was a Frenchman who knew some English. This man asked, 'What's wrong?'

'I just can't take it any more,' replied the British prisoner.

'Oh,' said the Frenchman, 'I think you can.'

'How do you think I can?'

'Well, I've been here,' he said, 'for five years.'

Sometimes the example of others might not exactly fit our own situation. They might have had to go through far more than us. Their giants might seem far larger than ours. We may not feel as if we can make five years, but, even if we are overwhelmed by our present battles, if they can do five years, maybe we could do two weeks or four weeks or more than we thought we could. So often, with a positive example to help frame our own experience, we realize we can go further than we could have ever gone before.

4. David sometimes needed support

Recently, when studying the story of David in the Bible, I came across a passage that is seldom referred to and which I had not come across before:

Once again there was a battle between the Philistines and Israel. David went down with his men to fight against the Philistines, and he became exhausted. And Ishbi-Benob, one of the descendants of Rapha, whose bronze spearhead weighed three hundred shekels and who was armed with a new sword, said he would kill David. But Abishai son of Zeruiah came to David's rescue; he struck the Philistine down and killed him. Then David's men swore to him, saying, 'Never again will you go out with us to battle, so that the lamp of Israel will not be extinguished.'[10]

There are only three verses here, but they highlight something important for us when it comes to facing our giants. When David fought Goliath, he stood alone in the strength of God when all around him were too afraid to face the giant. Here we are told that David, much later in life, comes to face 'the offspring of the titan'[11] or giant. In the New International Version (as above) and other translations, we are told that Ishbi-Benob was one of the descendants of Rapha. The word *raphe* in Hebrew elsewhere means 'giant', and in the Hebrew this word is preceded with 'the'. So rather than the descendant of Rapha, we have the descendant of 'the giant'. Perhaps, although I want to be clear that the passage doesn't directly make this connection, Ishbi-Benob is a descendant of Goliath.

Either way, here David comes face to face with another giant who seeks to take his life, but this time the battle doesn't go too well. This time David is older, more tired. This time it is the giant who has the upper hand, and David has to be rescued by Abishai. From that point on, David wasn't able or allowed to lead his troops into battle any more.

What is challenging here is that David is forced to accept that he needs help. He has to accept the support of Abishai; otherwise, the giant would have got the better of him.

There are times in our lives, as we face our giants, when we need support too. At such times, we acknowledge that we can't do it on our own, that the victory is won by strength in numbers and that this is a way that God can also use.

Speak to any alcoholic in recovery, and they will tell you that it is through the support of others that the giant is defeated. Speak to anyone who has had to wrestle with debt, and they will tell you that it is often through the support of others that the giant is defeated. Speak to someone who feels overwhelmed by depression, and they will tell you that through support they have found the giant to be defeated. There are some battles that we cannot, and should not, face alone. We need wisdom to know when we should seek support, or wisdom to know in advance to put support in place so that when the time comes, others can step in when we are struggling.

We need to recognize when we are 'exhausted', like David.

In many twelve-step programmes, people are encouraged to remember the acronym H-A-L-T to help them to recognize when they are *H*ungry, *A*ngry, *L*onely, and *T*ired – because when you start to feel these things, your ability to fight the giant becomes strained. You are in danger. It is then that you need to lean on the support of your Abishais, those who will step in and support you in the fight.

Who are those people who are for you? Who are the people you trust with your life, the ones who have stood beside you in the fight, and who you might need to ask to step in and fight alongside you again?

Remove the Ill-Fitting Armour

Then Saul dressed David in his own tunic. He put a coat of armour on him and a bronze helmet on his head. David fastened on his sword over the tunic and tried walking around, because he was not used to them.

'I cannot go in these,' he said to Saul, 'because I am not used to them.' So he took them off. Then he took his staff in his hand, chose five smooth stones from the stream, put them in the pouch of his shepherd's bag and, with his sling in his hand, approached the Philistine.[12]

Saul offered David his own armour. Imagine the prestige of wearing the king's armour – of going into battle wearing it, and everyone seeing the favour the king must have towards you!

It would have been very easy for David to simply accept Saul's offer and to gain all the kudos that came with it. Except for one simple matter: that kudos would have lasted a very short amount of time when Goliath dispatched David. He knew there would be no way for him to swing his sling while wearing this restricting gear. He would not be able to use the gifts that God had given him if he allowed this ill-fitting armour to remain.

So he made the brave decision to take it off.

There might be things that have been put on you over the years – perhaps words or attitudes – that you need to take off in order to walk in the anointing of God and face your giants.

It might be that you have been told you aren't worthy. That is ill-fitting on you because it was never meant to fit a person whom God has created and called 'worthy'.

It might be that you have been told you aren't good enough. That is ill-fitting on you because it was never meant to fit a person whom God has created and shaped as 'good'.

We carry around on our backs, every day, this ill-fitting stuff that we think gives us a hard skin that will protect us, but really it just weighs us down. It stops us from being able to walk in the calling that God has anointed us for, and we need to take it off. We need to learn to live in the freedom of the person God has created us to be. We need to stand in that, and be true to that.

The truth is that we find this really hard, mainly because we live in a culture of comparison where we strive to be like other people. We look at social media, and we see 'successful' people and we try to imitate them. We try to get that perfect shot for Instagram that makes us look like the perfect family on the perfect holiday, with the world's most photogenic and obedient dog, all while looking totally natural and spontaneous. We are frustrated and even fall out with one another as we try to choreograph our lives based on living up to the standards other people have set – as though they aren't facing the same challenges we are.

We can't be like other people. We can't wear their armour. We have to be ourselves. Not every job is a good fit for you, even if the pay is good. Your relationships with certain people will never be quite as you hoped, no matter how hard you work at them. That's just the way it is. We are all different, created differently. In this world, we have Sauls wearing armour, and we have Davids with shepherd's crooks.

It is significant that David took off Saul's armour, but it is also significant that David went down to the brook to get smooth stones for his sling. He operated in the gift that he had, rather than trying to imitate someone else. He was confident enough to stand as the person God made him to be. It is this self-confidence that endears us to David. He didn't have the self-doubt that Moses had; he knows that if he stays true to the person God has made him, and he trusts in God, then he will be victorious.

Be true to yourself. After all, God is the one who wired you the way you are. So why try to be someone you're not? That won't work for you any more than wearing Saul's armour worked for David. And could it be that Goliaths are not getting slain in your life simply because you're not fighting in a style that suits you?

With God We Have the Victory

As we think about facing our giants, I think that it is important for us to remember how this passage ends. The giant is defeated with God's help:

> As the Philistine moved closer to attack him, David ran quickly towards the battle line to meet him. Reaching into his bag and taking out a stone, he slung it and struck the Philistine on the forehead. The stone sank into his forehead, and he fell face down on the ground.
>
> So David triumphed over the Philistine with a sling and a stone; without a sword in his hand he struck down the Philistine and killed him.[13]

David was able to triumph over his giant because God was with him. That's the hope that David has, the hope we see right from the start: 'You come against me with sword and spear and javelin, but I come against you in the name of the LORD Almighty.'[14]

David cannot defeat Goliath on his own. It is because he is confident that the victory is God's that he is able to make his stand. For us, as we face our giants, we too can have confidence, not because of our own strength and our own ability to defeat them, but because we stand in the strength and victory of God.

Paul says these words to the church in Corinth: 'But thanks be to God! He gives us the victory through our Lord Jesus Christ. Therefore, my dear brothers and sisters, stand firm. Let nothing move you.'[15]

We all face giants in our lives! Do you still have yours in mind? At times they can feel really big, standing in front of us, unmoving, seemingly undefeatable. I can't tell you why there are some giants that we seem to wrestle with so much, and others that seem to be more easily defeated. Or why the ones we have to wrestle with and face up to seem to be so big, and why we sometimes have to face them for so long, even though the victory belongs to God. That's part of the mystery of faith, part of the tension we have to hold. But I do know that these words of Paul are true: 'What, then, shall we say in response to these things? If God is for us, who can be against us?'[16] And then later on: 'No, in all these things we are more than conquerors through him who loved us. For I am convinced that neither death nor life, neither angels nor demons, neither the present nor the future, nor any powers, neither height nor depth, nor anything else in all creation, will be able to separate us from the love of God that is in Christ Jesus our Lord.'[17]

Part of that victory is the knowledge that nothing can rob us of who we are in God. Nothing can separate us from the love we have in Jesus. As you think about those giants, as you think about facing them and how you might face them – even those giants that you have wrestled with for a long time – know that there is nothing about them that lessens in any way the love that God has for you. Know that there is nothing about them that in any way changes the identity you have as a child of God. Know that there is nothing about them that stops God from journeying with you through your life as you wait for his breakthroughs, and his mercy, his healing, his restoration or his victory.

As David came to the camp and saw the fear that the giant brought, listen to what he said to Saul: 'Let no one lose heart on account of this Philistine; your servant will go and fight him.'[18] This is what Jesus says to you today about that giant. He sees your struggle, he sees your fear, he sees your giant; and he says, 'Do not lose heart. I will go and fight him.'

It is not in our own strength and power that we will see the giants defeated. It is not in our own strength and power that we can overcome the fear that so often stops us from facing them. As David himself said to the Philistines: 'it is not by sword or spear that the LORD saves; *for the battle is the LORD's*, and he will give all of you into our hands.'[19]

There may be some who feel that when they come to faith in Christ, everything will be plain sailing. The truth is that even though we are in Christ, we are still in a battle; but the battle belongs to the Lord. God will give you the strength to overcome. The battle might be hard; it might be frightening; we might feel like the little shepherd boy standing in front of the towering giant . . . but just like David, with the Lord's strength, we too can persevere and overcome.

Without God, we live in fear that the giants will grind our bones to make their bread. Focused on God, we stand. Relying on our own strength, we fall. As Max Lucado says: 'Focus first, and most, on God. The times David did, giants fell. The days he didn't, David did.'[20]

As you read these words, perhaps God has been speaking to you about the giants you face. If so, then I'd like to encourage you to seek the support of someone you know and trust, and can be accountable to. Reach out to someone who can pray for you – perhaps for courage to be able to face your giants; or maybe for help if there are people around you who have been a discouragement in that battle; or maybe to ask for more of God's love to help you see who you really are in Christ, and to know more of his presence with you on that journey.

Notice that David found his best weapons in the river. When the Spirit of God is flowing through your life, like a mighty river or a gentle brook, it is often here, in the empowering of the Holy Spirit, that we find the best weapons with which to fight and overcome the enemy.

I have had to face giants in my life, on more than one occasion. I can assure you that the times I have fallen were the times when I tried to stand on my own. I was proud; I wanted to prove that I could manage, or cope, or overcome in my own strength. All of that was just a façade to cover over the hard reality that I just couldn't do it by myself. But in fact I wasn't meant to. David was confident because he had a God who stood with him and because he had an army standing behind him. If it had been only David standing in front of Goliath and the Philistine army, then we would be reading a very different story.

So, as you face your giants, may you know the power of the God who stands beside you; and may you know the encouragement and support of the army that stands behind you.

May you see your giants fall.

Questions for Reflection

1. Is the image of giants a useful one for thinking about situations in your life? If so, facing up to them is the first step in defeating them. What are your giants?

2. How can you make sure you are listening to the right voices in your life when facing your giants? Who is your Abishai who supports you when you need it?

3. What stories from your past can encourage you to keep on fighting your giants? Or other people's stories?

4. What armour are you using to fight your giants? Is that working for you, or do you need to ask the Lord for some new armour?

5. 'The battle is the Lord's.' What do you need to hear from God about how he sees you and how he helps you fight?

6. How can you encourage others when they face their giants?

3

Conflict

Conflict is inevitable. Every relationship, in any context, at some point in time will involve conflict. Whether it is your relationship with a spouse, or with children, or in the wider family; whether it is at work, or in church, or in your neighbourhood; wherever there is genuine depth of relationship there will be some form of conflict at some point.

The reason I mention this is so that we can recognize and acknowledge conflict when it comes, but also so that we might be able to move through it and resolve it in a healthy way.

Despite the presence of conflict in our lives, as I look among my books in my study I cannot find a single book that specifically deals with conflict resolution. And as I think back over a decade of preaching and teaching in the church, I struggle to think of many times I have taught about it outside of Matthew 18, which we will come to later.

I studied for three years at a Bible college, and again cannot remember many (if any) specific instances of teaching and training on this issue. Yet, when it comes to church life, rarely do I have to give people a coherent explanation of the ontological nature of the Trinity, but I do have to deal with conflict among them on a regular basis.

I do not want to give you a false picture of the church that I lead, because it is a wonderful community of people who deeply love one another and generally express that really well. That might seem like a contradiction – to be that kind of community but to still regularly experience conflict – but it simply highlights the lack of understanding we have surrounding conflict. Conflict is not merely defined as arguing or falling out. In fact, some people want to avoid that at all costs. Avoiding arguing, however, does not mean that you can or do avoid conflict. There are different ways to define it, but at its heart I believe conflict is a disharmony in relationship. It may be that one party is aware of this and the other isn't. It may be unspoken or even unidentified. The conflict is still there even if an argument hasn't broken out.

If I think about my relationships, wherever they may be, as places where I am genuinely committed to going deeper, to sharing more of myself and receiving more of the other person, then I have to accept that conflict is a reality I must learn to live with.

It was a reality that David knew all too well in his life too. In many ways David's life was one that was defined by conflict. David himself even reveals that this is the reason he is not able to fulfil his desire to build the temple for the Lord: 'But the word of the LORD came to me, saying, "You have shed much blood and have waged great wars; you shall not build a house to my name, because you have shed so much blood in my sight on the earth."'[1]

There is almost too much conflict in David's life for us to touch on in one chapter. What we can do is learn life lessons from the experiences of conflict in significant relationships in David's life, which can help us to enter into our own places of conflict.

Family – the School of Conflict

In the following discussion, some readers who are parents will relive a particular trauma they experienced, as we did, during the lockdowns of the coronavirus pandemic, so brace yourself. I am going to discuss . . . home-schooling.

This is a word that will live long in the memory. For some it is a way of life, for others it is a calling, for a few it is a necessity; but for a lot of people it will forever be associated with those several months which they wish never to return to, having developed a new-found respect and admiration for teachers.

While most of us accept that our children go to school to learn, we know that there is so much more that they learn in the home, and in many ways what they learn in the home is what shapes who they are as human beings, and how they get on in relationships, education, work and the wider world.

If you were to ask people where they experience conflict, and where that conflict is most painful and impactful, then I suspect that the answer would be one word: family.

I am sure that David, as the youngest of seven brothers, knew this to be true. As we have already seen in the previous chapter discussing the exchange between David and his brothers when he arrived at the Israelite camp, there was a typical sibling conflict running within David's family. I am also sure that this would not have been made easier by the anointing of the youngest, and the overlooking of the eldest, for kingship.

We see this often in the Bible when the youngest is chosen by God. We see it with Cain and Abel in Genesis 4; we see it with Esau and Jacob in Genesis 27; and we see it with Joseph and his brothers in Genesis 37. In all these instances the younger was chosen or blessed ahead of the older siblings, and in every case this caused tension and conflict. It caused Cain to murder Abel, it caused Esau to plan to murder Jacob and chase him from his home, and it caused Joseph's brothers to sell him into slavery and report the fake news of his death to their father.

Family is the school where we experience our primary lessons in conflict.

I have often come across people for whom this is true, but I rarely come across people who say that family life taught them how to deal with conflict well.

This could be for the best of reasons. Let me give you an example. As a child, I rarely saw or heard my parents argue, and conflict in their relationship was something that they kept away from us as children. In many ways that was right, but at the same time, it means the child doesn't get to see how conflict can be managed well. As I write this book, my parents are approaching their thirtieth wedding anniversary, and it has been a very happy thirty years. However, just as I said a moment ago, any relationship of depth will experience conflict. It is important not only to shield our children or family members from our conflicts where that is appropriate and best for them, but also to teach and model to them a healthy approach to conflict and conflict resolution.

So how can we do this?

1. Acknowledge that in relationship there needs to be flexibility

Within every family there are different relationship dynamics that function alongside one another. Within our home there are the dynamics between my wife Bex and me, between our son Leo and me, between Bex and Leo, between Bex and me as a parenting unit and Leo, and the three of us as three people within a household.

We are all different people, with different experiences of life and the world, and different ways of expressing ourselves, but we also live within a shared culture and environment which at its best is a place of nurture and safety for all of us.

Within this family environment there needs to be flexibility. Of course there are boundaries, and that is really important within family life. We have personal boundaries as individuals and we have collective ones as a family. Some of these involve how we deal with conflict.

The flexibility comes in understanding that my needs are not the only ones that need to be met within my family. My preferences are not the only preferences. My solutions are not the only solutions. As Charles Whitfield puts it: 'We may need to re-think and reframe our conflict from one in which it is "my way or the highway" (all-or-none) into one in which we entertain new possibilities that have otherwise been elusive.'[2] When we do this, we can see conflict and how we resolve it as an opportunity to learn and grow as individuals. We also learn how to love one another well as members of a family, and how to develop and maintain our homes as places of nurture and safety.

2. Keep working at it

There is an old saying: 'Nothing worth having comes easy.' This is true when it comes to our handling of conflict, especially if we want to handle it well. We have to keep working at it. I remember hearing an interview once on the radio with the leader of a Christian community, who was asked about how to maintain community. Her answer was: 'Community never arrives.' In other words, we have to keep working at it, keep seeking it, keep learning and growing and moving towards the other person.

It may be that you handled your last conflict really well. That's great. But rather than bask in that triumph, learn the lessons from it and commit to them for the next time round.

It may be that you handled your last conflict badly, or not as well as you had hoped. Don't beat yourself up. Learn the lessons from it and commit to them for the next time round.

Conflict is essentially about relationship. It isn't a matter of being right or wrong, even if there is someone who is right and someone who is wrong. It is always an opportunity to grow, an invitation to love, and a wake-up call that we need to keep doing that in order to deepen our relationships in the future.

Not all conflict comes within the home environment. There are wider issues of conflict we could look at, but almost always they revolve around a person.

As we look at the life of David, perhaps the most significant conflict he had, especially in the early part of his life, was with King Saul.

Saul and David had a complex relationship. They were king and subject, commander-in-chief and general, father-in-law and son-in-law, rivals, enemies. They both loved and hated each other.

Their relationship highlights for us the reality of conflict, but also gives us an insight into what we can avoid and do well when we face it.

What to Avoid in Conflict Resolution

There are life lessons that we can learn from this relationship between two kings, the present king and the future king, to help us as we seek to better understand our conflicts and better manage them.

Jealousy

Jealousy breaks up relationship and breeds mistrust.

> When the men were returning home after David had killed the Philistine, the women came out from all the towns of Israel to meet King Saul with singing and dancing, with joyful songs and with tambourines and lyres. As they danced, they sang:
>
> 'Saul has slain his thousands,
>   and David his tens of thousands.'
>
> Saul was very angry; this refrain displeased him greatly. 'They have credited David with tens of thousands,' he thought, 'but me with only thousands. What more can he get but the kingdom?' And from that time on Saul kept a close eye on David.[3]

Everyone loves the story of the underdog! As a football fan, I support Spurs (Tottenham Hotspur) and have done so for thirty years. Recently, in the FA Cup third round, my team was drawn against the Merseyside team Marine AFC, a minnow club in comparison from the eighth tier of English football. At the time of playing, there were 161 places between the two teams, the biggest gulf between two sides in the competition's 150-year history. This was truly the story of an underdog.

My mum sent me a message on the day of the fixture, asking if I was going to be watching and saying that she was hoping that Marine would win. I could see what she meant – because everyone loves the story of an underdog. I replied and said, 'On the one hand, yes . . . but on the other hand NO!' – because everyone loves the story of an underdog *except* the dog on top!

This is where we find Saul. David has come straight off the back of defeating Goliath. He has gone from a situation where almost nobody knew his name to now being known by everyone. Whatever he did, he was successful in it, and for Saul that was painfully difficult.

The fact was that Saul ruled by popular choice. Yes, he had been chosen by God, but his position had been created by the will of the people. As we have already seen, this had come about because Saul represented everything that they thought power and authority should look like. As soon as the popularity that Saul enjoyed switched to another, as soon as the praise of Saul was surpassed by another, Saul's jealousy took hold of him.

That jealousy drove a wedge between Saul and David because David became the focal point of Saul's downfall. Every bit of praise for David became a source of pain for Saul.

Have you ever been in that position? Have you ever felt as though a person around you, at home or at work, or in church, is getting all the things that you should get? How about the person who is praised constantly for what they do, and you know you do just as much as they do, but you don't get praised at all? Whether it is at work or at home, in church or at the social club, the trap of jealousy is always waiting to grab us. The common misconception with jealousy, though, is that the issue is with the other person. Look at how well *they* are doing; look at how praised *they* are. But jealousy is actually rooted in a struggle much closer to home, which is a sense of inadequacy in ourselves. The other person merely serves as a point of comparison for those inadequacies, but if you have ever struggled with a deep sense of inadequacy then you will know that you always manage subconsciously to seek out comparison with people who seem to have it better than you. The more this sense of comparison goes on, the longer we subconsciously seek out those we can feel 'cheated' by; and the more that sense of anger and bitterness grows inside us. We reach a point of feeling that every time the other person succeeds, every time they are praised, they are taking a piece of the pie that should have belonged to us.

That's when relationship breaks down, because that person now becomes a threat.

This culture of blame then seeps into the whole of our lives. We blame ourselves for not measuring up and we blame others for measuring up too much. In his book *The Blame Game*, Ben Dattner explores this issue really well. He reflects on how the world has changed over the generations.[4] He makes the distinction between the stick (blame) and the carrot (praise), and how in previous generations there might have been more of a focus on the former. Now we have much more of a focus on offering the carrot, on praising people, to help them grow and develop. As human beings, we are now much more conditioned to need praise. However, when reflecting on the world of work, Ben puts it like this: 'Many studies have shown that praise is in short supply in today's workplace.'[5] We are conditioned to receive praise, but we live in a world that does not always give it to us. This often leads to resentment or a sense of inadequacy, which can lead us down the road of jealousy.

Why mention this in a chapter on conflict? Because it is easy to see conflict, when it arises, as the fault of the other person. And there are times when that may well be true. But I genuinely believe that conflict would be much less of an issue if, when it arose, we spent a moment examining ourselves to be aware of our own feelings and where they are coming from. We may not avoid the conflict, but at least we can enter it with both eyes open. This also helps us to accept, and even in time celebrate, the achievements and successes of others, even if we wish they were our own.

The difference between Saul and Jonathan

There is a stark contrast in how Saul and Jonathan (Saul's son) deal with David.

Jealous Saul

Saul becomes jealous of David because of the fears and inadequacies within himself, and rather than taking a moment to process those things before God, he lashes out. We may wonder: what would Saul really have to be worried about, faced with this young, less powerful boy? After all, Saul was at the top of the tree; he was the king. But even at the top of the tree, you can be threatened into thinking that anyone climbing it is after your spot. Every rung they climb is a rung you slip down, or, as I have already said, every piece of the pie they have is one that is taken away from you.

Saul reaches a point, though, where the jealousy shifts: 'Saul became still more afraid of him, and he remained his enemy the rest of his days.'[6] He became afraid of David. He saw him as a serious threat to his position, and the conflict which had been bubbling beneath the surface broke out into a full-on war.

As Ian Coffey highlights: 'One of the most disturbing elements of this obsessive hatred of David is the way in which it escalates.'[7]

Saul has so many opportunities to deal with his growing anger and jealousy before it leads to conflict. He never takes them. He is either unable or unwilling to do the work that is needed: first to look at himself, and second, to reach out to David.

As is so often the case, the internal struggle spills out into external conflict. Saul is now determined to kill David. At the start of 1 Samuel 19, what has up until that moment been a lashing out becomes a premeditated plan of assassination: 'Saul told his son Jonathan and all the attendants to kill David.'[8]

David, even though he is son-in-law to the king, is a problem that needs to be got rid of; a threat that Saul's ego just can't handle any more. With the conflict no longer containable, in total Saul makes six attempts to kill David. Any sense of a former relationship is gone.

Loving Jonathan

However, we get a very different picture when it comes to Jonathan.

And in some ways this is surprising. Jonathan is Saul's eldest child and heir to this throne, so there is a strong degree of loyalty that exists between Saul and Jonathan, father and son, ruler and heir. In fact, Jonathan reveals the closeness of their relationship when later speaking to David about Saul's alleged plan to have David killed: '"Never!" Jonathan replied. "You are not going to die! Look, my father doesn't do anything, great or small, without letting me know. Why would he hide this from me? It isn't so!"'[9] Saul's relationship with Jonathan appears to be one of trust, at least from the perspective of monarch and heir. All that will change too with the conflict between Saul and David.

What we don't often realize is that Jonathan has just as much reason to be fearful and jealous of David as Saul does. If David is the one to replace Saul as king, then this means that Jonathan will miss out, be overlooked, be replaced. And yet, far from seeking to consolidate his power and position, Jonathan chooses instead to befriend David: 'And Jonathan made a covenant with David because he loved him as himself. Jonathan took off the robe he was wearing and gave it to David, along with his tunic, and even his sword, his bow and his belt.'[10]

Jonathan was well loved by the people,[11] so his friendship and protection of David is significant. But it is also costly, self-sacrificing friendship. He has popularity and power, but he uses them for the good of his friend. Every time Jonathan kept David safe or promoted his interests, he was harming his own chances of inheriting his father's throne. Jonathan's friendship with David came at the cost of his own career and harmed his relationship with his father.

There is a commitment between Jonathan and David which extends far beyond them both: 'Jonathan said to David, "Go in peace, for we have sworn friendship with each other in the name of the LORD, saying, 'The LORD is witness between you and me, and between your descendants and my descendants for ever.'"[12]

We will see this commitment honoured in a few chapters' time, but what strikes me here is that both David and Jonathan know that peace needs to continue beyond them. They knew that as rivals to the same throne, it was more than likely that their families and heirs could grow to hate one another and try to eliminate their opponents in the same way that Saul was trying to do. Their friendship and commitment to each other meant that they took steps to stop the cycle of rivalry and hate.

Despite every reason that Jonathan had to be jealous of David, he loved him. And in this we find the antidote to jealousy: relationship. When we see the other in love, it is much harder to feel bitterness towards them, and we can learn to celebrate their success and join others in praising them. We don't see their triumphs as detracting from our own, and so we are free to recognize both their and our own triumphs.

This is not always easy. There may be times when focusing on that relationship, or giving that love, is not only costly but gives us little in return: 'Jonathan lived out his covenant of friendship in circumstances that were anti-David . . . But the circumstances didn't cancel out the covenant; rather, the covenant was used in the purposes of God to overcome the circumstances.'[13]

Ultimately, if jealousy leads to conflict, then love can pull us back from it. Love can heal and restore even the most strained of relationships – if we are willing to bear the cost. It is not mere affection between Jonathan and David. It is a deep, self-sacrificing and committed love. It takes nothing less than this, for them and for us, to break the cycle of fear and jealousy.

Banishment

> Saul was afraid of David, because the LORD was with David but had departed from Saul. So he sent David away from him . . .[14]

Saul did what many of us do when it comes to conflict. He resorted to banishment. I don't think we would want to use the language of 'banishment', but essentially the sentiment is the same: we push the person away. Either through fear of them, or fear of what they provoke in us, we don't like how we feel with them around, so we push them away. In some cases, we even use banishment as a means of punishing. How many times do you send the dog to their bed when they've done something wrong? How many of us as children heard the words 'Go to your room', or 'Get out of my sight'? How many of us as parents still say that to our children?

As conflict arises and tension builds, there is always a temptation to push it away, along with the one we are in conflict with. There is a difference between needing space to calm down and then seeking to resolve the conflict, and banishment. There is a difference between stepping back and walking away. There is a difference between creating a calmer space where you can re-enter and isolating someone.

Pushing someone away rarely makes conflict less likely and it rarely makes relationship more likely. As creatures made for relationship, when we are deprived of it, we suffer.

It is important to realize that, in rare instances, breaking a bond is the healthiest thing to do, and the most needed. There are some relationships that cannot and should not last. If a relationship becomes toxic, abusive and completely without repentance, then it may be that God's grace is most clearly seen in the ending of that relationship. Conflict can be the means through which that reality is highlighted to us, and if a friendship or relationship has reached the end of the road, then it may well be that the time has come to say goodbye.

However, this is very different from banishing. We don't get the impression that Saul has worked through his feelings or resolved his issues with David. He just wants him out of the way. He doesn't want to have to deal with him. He wants him gone!

Saul's court, like many a court in the places of power throughout the ages, has 'cancel culture' at its heart. Anything, or any person, that is seen as unacceptable is eliminated. We may not hold court like Saul, but in our own lives there are times when we model this cancel culture. We 'ghost' people, ignoring them and cutting them out of our lives, sabotaging anyone we disagree with, rather than learning to conduct a healthy conversation and hold a difference of opinion.

I am sure that for most of us, there are people in our lives we feel that way about. Maybe not all the time, but on some occasions we are left wondering whether we would be better if that person wasn't around any more. When that feeling comes, rather than acting on it straight away, take some time to process and work through it.

Tension is something that we increasingly find hard to live with. We live in a world where technology and progress are designed to remove tension and stress from our lives. That's what we are told by the hundreds of advertisements and social media posts we see every day.

But tension, and conflict, as I said at the beginning of the chapter, are a natural part of human relationships. Making choices that are in the best interests of nurturing and maintaining relationships is not always easy. At times it is really hard.

For example, as parents Bex and I decided that sending Leo to his room was not the way we wanted to parent, because it simply conveys to him the message that we only want to be with him when he is happy and behaving nicely. This has meant we have had to work through the consequences of that choice. So, when he was a toddler and threw a tantrum, we would patiently sit with him, or at the very least stay in the room with him, sometimes for longer than we thought we could cope with, because we wanted to communicate the opposite message: *We are here with you because we love you, no matter what you are feeling or how you choose to express it.* We didn't want to abandon our child to face his most difficult emotions alone when he needed us there with him, right in the middle of what he was going through – as stressful and trying as it was at times.

Therefore, when conflict comes, and the temptation to push the other person away is great, just take a moment, take a breath. Create some temporary space if you need to; but if you do that, try to think through how and when you are going to re-enter the conversation, and clearly communicate this to the other person so they are not left feeling further abandoned and hurt.

In other words, don't let banishment, ghosting, cutting off, cancel culture (the list goes on) be the automatic response to conflict.

What to Try to Do in Conflict Resolution

Having looked at the relationship between Saul and David
and learned a couple of things to avoid when facing conflict,
we now move on to look at what positive things we might do
when conflict comes our way.

Find something of God in the other

> After Saul returned from pursuing the Philistines, he was told,
> 'David is in the Desert of En Gedi.' So Saul took three thousand
> able young men from all Israel and set out to look for David and
> his men near the Crags of the Wild Goats.
>
> He came to the sheepfolds along the way; a cave was there,
> and Saul went in to relieve himself. David and his men were far
> back in the cave. The men said, 'This is the day the LORD spoke
> of when he said to you, "I will give your enemy into your hands
> for you to deal with as you wish."' Then David crept up unno-
> ticed and cut off a corner of Saul's robe.
>
> Afterwards, David was conscience-stricken for having cut off
> a corner of his robe. He said to his men, 'The LORD forbid that I
> should do such a thing to my master, the LORD's anointed, or lay
> my hand on him; for he is the anointed of the LORD.' With these
> words David sharply rebuked his men and did not allow them to
> attack Saul. And Saul left the cave and went his way.[15]

This is a passage that has spoken to me over my time in pastoral
leadership. It has spoken to me in lots of different ways, but sig-
nificantly around the area of conflict. I especially remember my
years as an associate minister, working with a senior colleague

who was experiencing a number of health issues. There were some in the church at the time who were not being especially supportive of him, and who would arrange to see me and speak about how I should be leading the church. It was a very difficult period for us in leadership because we had developed a genuine warmth with our colleague and didn't feel that this small yet vocal minority was treating him fairly. There was a fine balance for me between picking up the slack when he was off work, and making sure that I wasn't stepping too much on his toes.

I tried during this time – and I feel I did this well – to honour and support my colleague in private as much as in public, when talking with those who disliked him (there are always some who dislike us as church leaders) as well as those who liked him.

This Scripture passage was firmly in my mind. Not because my relationship with this minister was anything like that between Saul and David; it clearly wasn't, and he did show great support for both Bex and me during our ministry there. The story came to mind because I believed that my colleague had been called to serve Jesus and this local church in the position of senior leadership, and I was not about to 'raise a hand', whether it was in words or in actions, against the Lord's anointed. Learning to honour another person, even in a place of conflict, is an important lesson. As Danny Silk remarks: 'The question is whether we will learn to use honour to navigate through conflict when it arises.'[16]

The interesting principle when we apply it to conflict more specifically is how we see something of God and ourselves in the other person.

David doesn't see Saul just as an enemy. He doesn't see him just as the person hunting him down. It would have been easy, right there in that cave, for David to have taken the throne. Here was his chance to get Saul out of the way. After all, David had been anointed by Samuel the prophet. Who was going to question his claim to the throne if he deposed Saul?

But David recognized that Saul had also been anointed by God through Samuel the prophet. In his commentary on 1 and 2 Samuel, Bill Arnold reflects on this moment: 'the anointed of Yahweh is endowed with Yahweh's Spirit and is therefore considered sacrosanct. The act of anointing itself imparts something of the sanctity of Yahweh to the anointed one, and the idea of striking such a one is repulsive to David.'[17]

What David sees, even in the middle of this conflict, is something of the Spirit of God within Saul. Because of the presence of God's Spirit, there is something holy about Saul; a circle that is drawn around him. We need to rediscover this mindset within our own conflicts.

Right at the very beginning of Genesis, we find a verse that is so challenging, so defining and so liberating that it is an amazement we skip over it so often. It is a verse that I keep being drawn back to, and it is one that we need to return to time and time again in situations of conflict:

> So God created humankind in his image,
>   in the image of God he created them;
>   male and female he created them.[18]

We are made in the image of God. People have debated what this means ever since it was written, and I don't want to wade into that debate other than to take it at face value. There is something in us, a spark, a blueprint, something woven into the very strands of our DNA and expressed ever so fragilely through our character, that reflects something of our Creator God.

Again, in the next chapter of Genesis in another account of the creation, we read: 'then the LORD fashioned the human, humus from the soil, and blew into his nostrils the breath of life, and the human became a living creature.'[19]

In the Hebrew language there is one word for spirit, breath and wind: the word *ruach*. So here, God breathes into the first human being the breath or Spirit of God.

As human beings, therefore, the very reason we exist is that God has breathed into us his Spirit, and our nature is to reflect and bear the image of God. For all of us, that capacity for reflecting and bearing is distorted by our failings, but our failings do not remove it. What we do can never remove who we are at this deep and fundamental level.

So when it comes to conflict, we need to learn to see God in the other, or at least to understand that the other too is created in love and in the image of God.

When you are struggling with a person, when you are in conflict with a person, I would like to invite you to do two things.

First, take those opening words of Genesis 1:27 and speak them out loud, adding in the name of the person you are in conflict with. I'll use my name as an example: 'So God created Andy in his image; in the image of God he created him.' Speaking out those words is significant because you are also hearing them back as you say them.

The second thing to do is to pray for the person. Seek God's blessing for them as a fellow human being created in the image of God. Ask God to breathe his Spirit freshly into them.

Perhaps then, the way you see the other person will begin to shift, and so will your conflict with them.

Not only does David see something of God in Saul, but he also sees something of himself. After all, David is also the Lord's anointed. There is a connection between David and Saul in their shared experience. They have both been taken from relative obscurity and thrust into the limelight. They have both been anointed by Samuel with holy oil and filled with the Spirit of God. Of all the people there in the cave that day, and in the kingdom at that time, Saul and David alone had this in common.

What are the things that you have in common with people when you find yourself in conflict with them? What are the points of connection? Can you see something of yourself in them?

Blink first – take responsibility

To end this chapter, I want to jump forward into the New Testament to some really significant and very practical teaching from Jesus on how to deal with conflict:

> If your brother or sister sins [against you], go and point out their fault, just between the two of you. If they listen to you, you have won them over. But if they will not listen, take one or two others along, so that 'every matter may be established by the testimony of two or three witnesses.' If they still refuse to listen, tell it to the church; and if they refuse to listen even to the church, treat them as you would a pagan or a tax collector.[20]

Whether conflict has come out of a sense of sin, or through some other means, this teaching is key to a healthy resolution of conflict in church communities, or families, or friendships.

It is a three-step process which seems easy and yet remains elusive in our strategies for conflict resolution.

Step one: 'Go and point out their fault . . .'

This is perhaps the hardest step of all, and isn't that true for so many things in life! Resolving conflict requires something of us. This is our responsibility. However, there are two parts to this first step.

First, there is the physical action of going. This takes courage and humility, and, as it did with Jonathan, it takes a focus on the relationship. What the passage explains to us is that the purpose of going is to 'win over' the person you are in conflict with. Our motivation is key here, because if we go with an attitude of 'being in the right', we are unlikely to win anyone over.

It is so easy for us to think, especially if we believe that the other person is in the wrong, that he (or she) is the one who needs to take the first step. He/she is the one who is in the wrong so he/she is the one who needs to take on the responsibility of making things right. Right? Wrong! Jesus says that even if you are the one who has been wronged, it is you who needs to go. Here is the thing: it requires us to go *personally* – not write a letter, or send an email, or apologize by text message. Go in person. As William Barclay said in his commentary on this passage: 'The spoken word can often settle a difference which the written word would only have exacerbated.'[21]

Second, we are to point out the other person's fault. Again, this is not easy. It takes courage to be able to put into words the nature of our complaint, and it also requires us to acknowledge that there is a problem. We are not always ready to do this. I was reminded recently that perhaps the reason we are reluctant is because acknowledging the problem means I have to do something about it! If Jesus requires me to go in the spirit of winning over the other person, then ignoring the issue means I don't have to do anything. This seems so much easier. Except that it isn't, because what is happening beneath the surface of our inactivity is that the anger, hurt and wound begins to grow, stir and fester. Any wound that we leave unattended will in the end cause us harm. Even the smallest of wounds can end up having a big effect on the rest of the body. A quote that I have often found helpful is one I saw once on social media and sadly have not been able to find a source for. What it says, though, is really telling: 'If you don't heal what hurt you, you'll bleed on people who didn't cut you.'

You may feel as though doing nothing isn't harmful, and you may even be OK with sacrificing your own health and happiness by not dealing with the conflict, although I would strongly urge you not to go down that road. But be aware that there are others who are affected by the issue as well. How many times has an unresolved conflict spilled over into the relationships around you? It can affect the way you speak to your spouse, your children, your colleagues or generally people around you. What you're doing is bleeding on people who didn't cut you, because you are refusing to acknowledge that there is a wound and refusing to take the responsibility for treating it.

So for your own good, and for the good of those around you, go and point out the fault of the other person, that you may win them over!

Step two: 'Take one or two others along . . .'

What I like about this passage is that Jesus acknowledges in his teaching that not every relationship can be healed, not every conflict resolved, at the first attempt. Sometimes you try your best, you do the right thing, you take responsibility and go, you lovingly point out the issue . . . and the other person doesn't budge. They haven't met you in the same spirit that you have met them. What do you do next? Give up? Say, 'I've done what was required of me – the ball's in their court'? No! The responsibility is still on you, but it is not on you alone. It's time to bring some others along with you.

There are two pieces of advice I would give when thinking about who to bring with you.

First, make sure that they are people who know both of you, if possible, and are committed to resolving the conflict. Don't just choose people who are 'on your side'. Taking 'your friends' into a situation of conflict could be seen by the other person as your attempt to send in the cavalry. But bringing '*our* friends' to a situation of conflict can create a bridge between you on which to meet.

Second, choose people who you know will be honest with you; and be prepared to hear some home truths from them as well. It might be, even as you are highlighting the faults of the other person, that you have some faults of your own that need to be highlighted. So choose people whom you love and respect enough to take that kind of counsel from them.

There are always two sides to every conflict, but it is not always easy to see the faults on our own side. If you are genuinely interested in seeing the conflict resolved, then it might be that you too need to make some changes, or make amends. Perhaps before taking this step, speak to those friends and ask them to be honest with you during and after the meeting so that they know they have permission to speak candidly and openly in this way; but also pray that God would give you a spirit of humility, and ears to hear those words if they come. As it says in Proverbs: 'Wounds from a friend can be trusted . . .'[22]

Step three: 'Tell it to the church'

This command may be specific to the Christian community, but I think it applies to communities more widely too. Life and relationships are not lived in isolation; they are lived in community. We are not separate streams, but currents flowing within wider streams, and so what affects one relationship will affect others. Or, since Paul uses the analogy of the body in 1 Corinthians 12 and Romans 12, what affects one part of the body affects the other. A while ago I injured my knee and had to have lots of investigative work done by specialists to get to the bottom of the problem. In the end it was down to some tendon damage, but the issue in my knee also made my feet sore. Because I was walking differently, the impact was felt in another area of my body. When we experience conflict within one part of 'the body', we walk differently, and that impact is felt by the rest of the body. It makes sense, then, that resolving that conflict is the responsibility of, and in the interests of, the whole body.

I have only once had to get to this stage within a church community, and there were specific things that we did as a church to make sure that even at this stage we were focused on restoring the relationship and winning the person over. Winning the person is always more important than winning the argument. I would therefore strongly suggest the following actions.

First, make it clear to the person again that your desire is to live in a restored and positive relationship with them.

Second, review the process. Explain that you have followed steps one and two, but that this has not achieved the restoration of the relationship.

Third, explain why you feel it is necessary that you take step three. Perhaps use the image of the body.

Fourth, manage what you say. Ideally, it is important that the other person is there to hear what is said but is also allowed to speak for themselves. In the case of the person in my example, it wasn't easy to get the person to meet us, so we made every effort to make it as easy as possible. In the end, they refused to come, so we had to make sure we managed what we said to keep it as fair and as balanced as possible. We wrote a statement which would be read to the church, covering the three points I have just mentioned, and sent a copy to the person involved. Along with it I wrote a letter explaining to this individual that I would read the statement to the church in our members' meeting, and say nothing else. This way they knew exactly what was going to be said.

We prayed as a church that the situation would be resolved, and I explained to the church that it was the responsibility of all of us to work towards the restoring of that relationship.

It was a slow and at times difficult road. But in the end, there was some level of reconciliation made between the people involved and between the person at fault and the church community. Either way, what we modelled in our process was our desire to deal with conflict in a helpful and healthy way, following the principles laid out by Jesus.

Step four: a step too far?

There has been much debate about what to make of this last part of the teaching: 'if they refuse to listen even to the church, treat them as you would a pagan or a tax collector.'[23]

Some think that this teaching was added to the words of Jesus later by the church.[24]

Some emphasize the need to exclude a person from community activity.

However, what this step highlights is that relationship can only be restored on the other side of conflict. If you have gone through steps one to three and the person still refuses to be won over, you have done everything that is required of you, and so has the community. The choice then to live outside of fellowship remains with the one who has refused to be won over, who has refused to be reconciled. Perhaps, therefore, this is a time to step back and to allow that person to live with the consequences of the choices they have made.

There were other conflicts in the life of David, and other lessons that could be learned from how he dealt with them. He, like you and I, did not always deal with conflict well, and there were times when his relationships suffered as a result. Either way, he is a person from whom we can learn a lot, both what to do and what not to do, as we live within the reality of conflict.

As for David and Saul, their relationship reached a settled point. Perhaps we couldn't go so far as to use the word 'reconciliation', but it was certainly a point where conflict ceased.

It wasn't easy for David. It was costly, as it is for us. But if we are to be a people who have a heart that reflects God, perhaps there is no other way to resolve the conflicts we face.

When Jesus is on trial before Pilate, he is asked the question 'Are you a king?' His reply is telling: 'My kingdom is not of this world. If it were, my servants would fight to prevent my arrest by the Jewish leaders. But now my kingdom is from another place.'[25] What Jesus is implying here is that the nature of the kingdom should be seen in the behaviour of his followers. His followers do not behave as the world behaves.

So it is our responsibility, as those who follow Jesus, to learn how to model these important life-skills well – not just for our own personal benefit but also for the good of the whole: for our children, our communities, and for those watching and learning from us in all walks of life. It is part of our witness to a God of peace and reconciliation.

These things are not easy to learn and are costly to put into practice, as well as grow from them. But it is only with practice and encouragement from one another, and a firm belief that these issues are important, that we will be able to cultivate and model them as part of our witnessing arsenal.

No one is born good at any skill. We must work hard to develop them – but what a harvest is to be reaped when we do!

Questions for Reflection

1. How was conflict dealt with in your family when you were growing up? As an adult, do you deal with it in the same way?

2. Looking at the story of Saul and David, what causes jealousy and how does it lead to conflict? Do you relate to their story?

3. Thinking of Jonathan, how does relationship beat jealousy?

4. Cutting people off isn't the answer to conflict. Why not?

5. Think of someone with whom you are in conflict. What good things can you think about them? What can you pray for them?

4

The Waiting Game

I don't know how good you are at waiting for things?

There are times when I can be quite patient, and other times when my patience wears thin. The place where I am least patient, where I really don't like to wait, is in the car. Stand me in a line in a supermarket and I seem utterly serene, but if I am in a queue in the car stuck in traffic then my patience seems to evaporate fairly quickly.

Perhaps you are someone who finds the supermarket queue a place where your ability to wait is tested? Scanning along to see which queue is moving quickest, and then with the speed and skill of Lewis Hamilton, you shoot across the supermarket with your trolley, weaving among families, staff and the produce to get you to the hallowed ground of a faster-moving queue, only to get out of the shop one minute quicker.

That is exactly what I am like, but in a car. So if I am on a motorway and I hit traffic, I'm looking for the fastest-moving lane, and it always seems to be, through some cruel trick of the universe, that the lanes I am not in are the ones that are moving faster. Then I make the bold decision to step out in faith and change lanes . . . and that lane slows down. Maybe God is trying to teach me something about patience and waiting.

I heard a story recently about a man's great-grandfather at the turn of the twentieth century. This man was trying to cook eggs outdoors over an open fire and became impatient with how long it was taking. Bear in mind as you read this that eggs, of all the things that you can cook, don't take very long, so you will have an idea of the man's level of patience. He decided that he needed to speed the process up, and nothing does that better on a fire than adding more fuel, so he doused the fire with kerosene. The flames roared into life, badly burning not just the eggs but the man's face. He then had to go to casualty where, you've guessed it, he had to wait . . . to get his burns treated.

Waiting Is Hard

Waiting is something we often struggle with. The context might look different for each of us, but I think if you give it some thought, you'll be able to call to mind something that tests your patience, or an area of your life where you don't like waiting.

What does this have to do with the story of David? After all, David wasn't dashing across the supermarket shoving a trolley in front of him, or weaving through the lanes of the M5. But David was well schooled in the art of waiting.

A couple of chapters ago we saw how David was anointed in Bethlehem by Samuel, and while we are not told David's age exactly, some scholars think he was merely a boy, between 10 and 15 years of age at that moment. As we've already explored, this is a pivotal event, where David is chosen above the rest of his family, above the rest of the nation, to be the next 'chosen one'.

And then, as we saw in Chapter 2, David went on to slay the mighty giant Goliath, and it seemed as though the story of David was taking on an unstoppable momentum and that everything was lining up well for him.

However, at the start of 2 Samuel we read that David had to wait until he was 30 years old to become king.[1] That's somewhere between fifteen and twenty years from his anointing to his coronation. There are twenty chapters between 1 Samuel 16 (the anointing) and 2 Samuel 5 (the coronation), and while we can't explore all of that history in this chapter, there are lessons that David learned in that time which can both encourage and challenge us today, as we too learn to play the waiting game.

The longer the waiting goes on, the harder it becomes. Most of us, after a significant amount of time, might give up and feel as though the anticipated event is just never going to happen. Imagine that you went for an interview in your place of work, and you were told by your boss that you were the person they believed was going to take the company forwards, and that they had a lot of faith in you, and that you were going to get the new senior position with all the responsibility and perks. You would be feeling pretty excited, I imagine. You would get on the phone and tell your family and friends about your big news. But what would you do if after a week nothing had happened, and you hadn't heard anything? You might be able to reassure yourself by saying, *Well, they're probably just sorting out the contract, and I won't ask because I don't want to seem too pushy*. But what if after a month nothing had happened? Or six months, or a year? You might think, *Well, I suppose they're preparing me or grooming me for this position, and that's why it has taken such a long time to get things moving*.

But if after twenty years you still hadn't heard anything, and the promotion still hadn't happened, then you would feel as though it was never going to happen. Because waiting, especially over long periods of time, is hard. That's exactly the kind of wait that David knew.

Maybe those were the thoughts that David had at various points along the way: *Is it ever going to happen? Will I ever be king?*

We have certainly learned a thing or two about waiting recently, haven't we? During this time of the Covid-19 pandemic we have all been through a painful lesson in waiting. Waiting to see family and friends whom we haven't seen for months; waiting to grieve family and friends we have lost but not been able to properly say goodbye to; waiting to be able to leave the house without fear; waiting to be able to enter a shop or public place without having to wear a face mask; waiting to sing in church; waiting for the kids to go back to school.

We had to learn to wait outside supermarkets in those early days because there were huge queues of people snaking around the car parks, which I imagine was really tough on those itchy-footed queue-swappers among us. The one thing, happily, that we didn't have to wait in during those early days was a traffic jam, because there wasn't anything on the roads, which brought some joy to me in those difficult months of spring 2020.

We are told that 20/20 vision is desirable, and due to the Covid-19 pandemic we all had to develop 20/20 vision, but that vision was long-distance.

Earlier this year I had a much more painful lesson in waiting than any of my experiences at the supermarket or on the motorway. On one of the days when I had set aside time to write, I had quite a bad headache. That's not something that would usually bother me, but as the day went on I lost the sense of feeling in my right arm and felt quite unwell. When I got home later in the day, Bex saw that I wasn't feeling great and encouraged me to speak to someone on the NHS 111 service. After a short conversation a priority ambulance was called, I was given a few short moments to say goodbye to my wife and son, and I was rushed to the Royal United Hospital in Bath with a suspected stroke. Given that both my father and sister had died from strokes at a younger age than I am, it was a very worrying time for all of us.

While on the Acute Stroke Unit I was given an MRI scan, and after waiting for the results for most of that next day, a doctor came to deliver the verdict: I had not had a stroke. That was amazingly good news for all of us, but at that moment, with my symptoms having eased, it was an outcome I was expecting. What I was not expecting was what came next: 'We have found two growths on your brain, a smaller one around half a centimetre in diameter, and another around three centimetres in diameter. We will need to investigate these further.'

Within the hour, I was discharged from hospital with all manner of tests and scans booked in for the coming weeks.

As the tests came and went, and we waited for the results, I learned painfully that waiting is hard. Was I OK – or not? There was no word either way from the medical team. I remember several people telling me that 'no news is good news', to which I often replied, frustrated, 'No. No news is *no* news.'

Waiting for scans and the results of those scans, especially when they weren't conclusive, was hard because of what it brought out of us all. For me, it was fear. *What if I'm not OK? Will I get to see my son grow up? Will I leave my wife behind as a single parent?*

A couple of chapters ago we looked at how David overcame Goliath. I remember reflecting, as I listened to the song 'Goliath' by Lucy Grimble, that these growths on my brain were not my giant to overcome; they were simply the battlefield on which the struggle was taking place. Fear was my Goliath. I was trying to not give in to fear; trying to take every thought captive and to live in the moment; trying not to worry until we were given a reason to worry.

What the doctors diagnosed in the end was not immediately serious; the growths were benign cysts which would need to be monitored on a regular basis in the years to come.

In reality, the waiting for results and answers wasn't all that long: a few months. However, in the moment it seems so much longer. When everything is up in the air, it feels like an age.

We look at the story of David, and we think, *Well, twenty chapters – that's not too long*. Or we think, *Fifteen years – that's not too bad. After all, he's only a boy*. We can do this because we know where the story ends up – we've already read to 2 Samuel 5. But do you know who didn't know, who hadn't got there yet? David! David was living it, and for him it must have seemed like an awfully long time. For us, when we look back on this pandemic, in the grand scheme of things it might be that it wasn't all that long, only a year or so, but at the time, when we were living it, it just didn't feel like that.

The Odds Are Never in Your Favour

There are also mindsets within our society which make waiting hard. If we find it hard to wait as individuals, then it is partly because we are told by our culture that waiting is bad. Or at the very least we can be preyed upon by a society that exploits our dislike of waiting.

Instant satisfaction

Our culture encourages us to be instantly satisfied. Waiting is seen as robbing you of the joy you could experience in having the thing you want *now*. If you wonder to what extent this is true within our society, think of it this way. Companies, whose sole purpose is to make money, will actually give you money in the form of credit, so that you can have the things you want instantly rather than having to wait for them. As a society we go for that because we get to have what we want, but the odds are not stacked in our favour. While you are enjoying your purchase instantly, you are having to pay for that privilege for longer, and more of us are doing just that. According to one debt advice firm, 'more than half of UK consumers (approximately 27 million people) entered the year 2020 while being in debt'.[2]

One comparison site highlighted our embracing of this way of life over the past thirty years. In the spring of 1993, the total amount spent on credit cards in the UK was £2.9 billion. A decade later, in May 2003, it had trebled to £10 billion and by October 2018 it had almost doubled again to £18.45 billion. In under thirty years, UK credit card spending had increased sixfold.[3]

There is nothing wrong with buying something on credit. In fact there are lots of different types of finance that rely on it; student loans and mortgages are examples. And the reasons we use credit cards vary too, such as buying food or other essentials to tide us over until our next payday, or covering our utility bills; and some people use them for the insurance benefits included with more expensive expenditures such as booking a holiday. The challenge is that it can become easy to lean on credit, allowing it to take hold of us, because we don't like to wait. Perhaps this increasing trend in our culture should give us cause to stop for a moment and think to ourselves, *Do I really have to have this now? Perhaps it might do me good to wait for it, to save for it?*

Nothing is new under the sun . . . and even in the news

We live in a world that has 24/7 news coverage. Here in the UK we have a free news channel called BBC News 24, where the news runs on a 24-hour loop. In fact, everything is caught up within this day-long cycle, from the news we watch on TV, to the entire repository of human knowledge at our fingertips on our smartphones, to our relational engagements through social media. Everything is instant and at our fingertips. It doesn't even need to be new for us to engage with it. We will look at the same content again and again, listen to the same news stories again and again, get caught up in the cycle day after day . . . simply because it is there. I don't need to wait to see my friends in order to know what is going on with them – I can literally see what they had for breakfast because they posted a picture of it twenty minutes ago. I don't need to wait until the 10 o'clock news on TV tonight because I can see the headlines right now on my browser home page. We are used to being able to have access to what we want, and who we want, when we want it/ them. We are prepared to put up with out-of-date information simply because it is there now.

So here is a challenge in waiting. Why not stop looking at the news throughout the day and instead watch the evening news headlines, or simply check the news once a day? Why not stop spending ages looking at the same pictures of your friends throughout the week, and instead wait until the end of the week and give them a call?

It is in choosing to wait, little by little, within this fast-paced culture, that we reclaim our society, one little act of rebellion at a time.

Wasted time

Our society often labels time when we are not getting what we want, or not doing what we want, as 'wasted time'. Unproductive time is described as wasted time because our use of time has to have an outcome in order to be deemed valuable. This is a real challenge in our society, and we see it creeping in to the lives of our children too. We feel the need to fill their days with activity, or to manage their activity because we don't want to waste the time we have with them or their opportunity to develop. But there is something important, both developmentally and socially, about 'wasted time' or 'boredom time'. For one thing, it sparks both imaginative and creative processes within our children. When we are free and given space, then we can choose to make the most of that space. We have to think how we want to fill that space.

That period of time, when it seems like nothing is happening, or nothing of note, far from being wasted time, is actually really significant. In one of my previous books, *Infused with Life*, I looked at how our culture can often view rest as 'dead time' because nothing productive comes from it.[4]

What both concepts – wasted time and dead time – highlight is that our culture has a very narrow view of productivity.

If you are sitting reading this and feeling that you struggle with waiting, then hopefully this has shown you that our culture plays on that, or certainly doesn't help you. It can sometimes feel as though the odds are never in your favour when it comes to waiting in this instantly gratifying, slow-news, boredom-phobic society that only values what you can see or produce.

But what if the measure of our time wasn't so much about what we could 'get' at the end of it, but about *who* we became through our approach to it? What if we viewed waiting, not as a waste, but as an opportunity to be seized, or a chrysalis to enter into?

Don't Waste the Wait

If we look through the Bible, we often come across great people of faith who have to spend significant portions of their time waiting.

Abraham and Sarah are promised a son by God but have to wait decades before God fulfils that promise and Isaac is born. There must have been moments, as the years rolled by and they got older and older, when Abraham thought the promise of God was not going to come to pass. It got to the point, when the promise was confirmed, that it was laughable:

> Then one of [the angelic visitors] said [to Abraham], 'I will surely return to you about this time next year, and Sarah your wife will have a son.'
>
> Now Sarah was listening at the entrance to the tent, which was behind him. Abraham and Sarah were already very old, and Sarah was past the age of childbearing. So Sarah laughed to herself as she thought, 'After I am worn out and my lord is old, will I now have this pleasure?'[5]

It was a painful laugh. A laugh tinged with sadness. A laugh betraying the loss of hope and the presence of too many 'what-might-have-beens'. Waiting was hard.

But then a year later, the laughter turned to joy as God fulfilled his promise and Isaac was born. The name Isaac means 'laughter'.

Jacob falls in love with Rachel, but he can't just marry her – he has to work for seven years for her father before he can take her as his wife. Even then he gets tricked into marrying the other daughter and has to work another seven years to marry Rachel. So Jacob has to wait fourteen years to marry the woman he loves. There must have been a moment, having worked seven long years, when the prospect of another seven – knowing how long that wait had been – discouraged Jacob. If it did, it didn't put him off. Rachel was worth waiting for.

There may be times in our lives when we know from past experience exactly what that waiting means, and this can be discouraging. But it can also encourage us: we know that we can live through the waiting time again because we have done it before.

Joseph had to wait in prison. We tend to get disoriented by the fast pace of Joseph's story and miss the timescale: he was in prison for thirteen years. There must have been times during the cold, dark nights in prison when Joseph wondered if he was ever going to see the light of day. Had God forgotten him? How did all of this fit in to God's plan and purpose? Those dreams must have seemed a long way away and a long time ago. But Joseph keeps faithful to who he is, and during the waiting he helps those around him.

Jesus is around the age of 30 when he begins his public ministry. In Matthew's gospel we read what happens at the very start of that ministry, at his baptism: 'As soon as Jesus was baptised, he went up out of the water. At that moment heaven was opened, and he saw the Spirit of God descending like a dove and alighting on him. And a voice from heaven said, "This is my Son, whom I love; with him I am well pleased."'[6]

Again, we may wonder: what was it that God was pleased with? Perhaps, among other things, Jesus didn't waste the wait. He wasn't sitting around simply waiting for things to fall into his lap. He lived a good life and was a contributing member of his community. He didn't need to be famous to be faithful, and so what pleases God is how Jesus lived in those waiting years. It is in these years that he was moulded and shaped and grew into the man that God had created him to be.

It was the same for David. Yes, he was a man after God's heart because of who he was as king, but he was also a man after God's heart because of how he allowed God to shape him and raise him, not just in the fame moments but in the faithful moments. Often we fall short, we struggle, not because we neglect the fame moments, the up-the-front moments, but because we neglect the faithful moments, the behind-closed-doors moments.

It was also in this time that David learned.

He learned courage when he had to face Goliath.

He learned how to submit to authority, even when that authority wasn't good, during his conflict with Saul.

He learned to lead in this time. He learned what it meant to be humble. But most importantly of all, he learned to trust God; to trust that God would bring about what he promised. He grew in the understanding that God was a God who finished the things he started. It was a promise that Paul had to learn too, and he shares what he has learned with the Philippians: 'In all my prayers for all of you, I always pray with joy because of your partnership in the gospel from the first day until now, being confident of this, that he who began a good work in you will carry it on to completion until the day of Christ Jesus.'[7]

God is doing something in your waiting too: God is shaping you to be the woman or man that he has made you to be. Waiting might not be what we want, but it might be exactly what we need.

What is it that you are waiting for? Whatever it is, don't simply think of that time as dead time, but instead allow it to be used productively. Proactively open your heart to God and allow yourself to be shaped, moulded, developed and refined by him, because when we are open to that, the person who arrives at the end of the waiting is much more able to embrace what they waited for.

In Psalm 27 David says:

> Wait for the LORD;
>> be strong and take heart
>> and wait for the LORD.[8]

Don't Skip the Wait

It is easy, when we feel as though God is asleep at the wheel, to reach over and try to give him a helping hand. There is a phrase that has been used a lot in the past few years here in the UK, and it will provoke different responses in different people: 'take back control'. That was part of the argument for the 'leave' campaign during the Brexit process, and however we voted in that referendum, and whatever feelings that phrase evokes in us, that is the temptation we all face. When things are not going as we like, or when it feels as though we are having to wait for longer than we want, the temptation is to take back control.

The argument about control in the Brexit process wasn't so much about control as it was about powerlessness. Control seemed to be the antidote to powerlessness. For us, as we struggle to live with waiting, sometimes it's not the waiting that really challenges us; it's the powerlessness. When I am waiting, I feel powerless. I am not able to bring about the thing I am waiting for; I am not able to make it happen, no matter how much I want it.

And that sense of powerlessness is compounded when the power lies with someone else. We call out to God because we believe that God has no lack of power. After all, when you are feeling powerless, who better to call out to than the one who made the stars? But often we do not find that easy, even, at times, with God, because we would much rather keep our grip on the things we are striving for than admit that there is nothing, or very little, that we can do to change our situation. And yet this is exactly what the Scriptures call us to do – to let go.

We often quote the well-known words from Psalm 46: 'Be still, and know that I am God.'[9] However, there is an argument for translating these words as: '*Let go*, and know that I am God.' The Hebrew verb means to relax your grip on something.[10]

It is terribly hard to let some things go, even when we give them over to God. Perhaps it is a dream that you have longed for over many years that just hasn't materialized, but neither has it gone away; or an illness that you have had to live with, but you long for healing. Many of us know the ache in our hearts of dreams we still wait to see become reality. We grip those dreams tightly, because to let go of them can feel like a loss. But letting them go is not dropping them into the misty void of the always-just-out-of-reach; it is entrusting the precious threads of those hopes to our loving heavenly Father, and asking him to weave them into his glorious tapestry in his way and in his time. It's hard, and the end result might look different from what we imagined, but there is no safer person to entrust our dreams to than the original dreamer himself, and there is no safer place to be powerless than in the arms of our almighty heavenly Parent. What are you waiting for? What is it that you need to let go of and put into his hands today?

It can be especially hard if you are the kind of person who likes to get out there and make things happen for yourself – to grab the bull by the horns. Or maybe you are surrounded

by people like that? David was, and we read about them in
2 Samuel 23:

> At that time David was in the stronghold, and the Philistine garri-
> son was at Bethlehem. David longed for water and said, 'Oh, that
> someone would get me a drink of water from the well near the
> gate of Bethlehem!' So the three mighty warriors broke through
> the Philistine lines, drew water from the well near the gate of
> Bethlehem and carried it back to David. But he refused to drink
> it; instead, he poured it out before the LORD. 'Far be it from me,
> LORD, to do this!' he said. 'Is it not the blood of men who went at
> the risk of their lives?' And David would not drink it.[11]

As an aside, I feel I might have been pretty put out if I was one
of the three mighty warriors who had found their way through
enemy lines to get David a drink, only to see him pour it on
the ground. It highlights both their loyalty to David and the
fact that these were guys who liked to make things happen.
There was no talk of being patient: 'Let David wait until we
can safely get him some water.' And we see this attitude again
in the story we recounted in the previous chapter, describing
the time when David and Saul are in the cave at En Gedi (see
1 Sam. 24). When Saul happened to wander into the cave
where David and his men were hiding, he must have looked
like manna from heaven, placed by God into their waiting
mouths. In fact, that's pretty much what the warriors tell
David in verse 4: 'The men said, "This is the day the LORD
spoke of when he said to you, 'I will give your enemy into
your hands for you to deal with as you wish.'"'

David, in sparing Saul, does not just choose to see something of God's Spirit within him or even something of himself;

he also chooses to give up control. He chooses to let go, and to entrust the precious threads of his hopes into the hands of his loving heavenly Father, asking him to weave them into his glorious tapestry in his way and in his time. David waits. He lets go of the sword handle and he places his future in God's hand. He doesn't waste the wait, but he doesn't skip the wait either.

Even God Has to Wait

The amazing thing is this: as we, like David, learn this life lesson of waiting, we also see that God waits. God has to wait for his dream.

God might not wait as we wait, and time for God of course is different from time as we experience it, but if you think about it, God has been waiting far longer than us to see his deepest desire come to pass.

From the beginning, God had a shining dream in his heart that he would share his creation with his children. Adam and Eve walked in the garden with God, enjoying a closeness and intimacy that we will not know this side of eternity. As people, though, we have been distracted, and like a miner coming across fool's gold, the eyes of our hearts have been turned by what seems to glitter but is not gold. Still the eyes of our hearts are easily turned, not by a well-chosen piece of fruit but by the constant bombardments of life, by our desires and by a faith that often promotes the institution of church over discipleship and relationship.

Has God given up on his dream? When all seemed to be lost, and human beings had turned their back on him and walked away, did God skip the wait? No. In fact, Paul reminds us that 'when the set time had fully come, God sent his Son . . .'[12]

God waited for the right moment. He didn't rush in. If there was purpose to his timing, then there was purpose to his waiting. And when the time was right, God stepped in.

God does not skip the wait, but neither does God waste the wait. If God had wasted the wait for the time to be right, then we wouldn't have the Old Testament, which is packed full of how God used that time to prepare us for when that time was right. Through the prophets and judges, through poets and kings, through suffering and prosperity God didn't waste a minute to speak to us of his love, to reassure us that there was purpose in his timing and purpose in the waiting.

What about now? Sometimes we wonder, *what is God waiting for?* Does God waste the wait now? No. Just as before, he doesn't miss a moment to prepare us for what will be, for what is coming, for who we will be. He prepares us for what it will be like when we walk in the cool of the garden with him once again. He prepares our hearts for a world where there will be no glittering distraction but only the radiant shining of his face. He prepares us to share in the reality that we were always made to live within – intimate and close relationship.

Do you think that is worth waiting for? God thinks so.

If God can wait for his dream of a restored creation, when he can again walk in the cool of the garden with us, then perhaps we can learn to wait too. Perhaps our prayer can move from 'Help me get through the waiting' to 'Teach me what it means to wait as you wait.' We can ask to learn what *holy waiting* is, where we do not see ourselves as being stuck in isolated moments or enduring the ticking down of a clock towards what we think we want; but rather we see ourselves as caught up within the times and seasons of the one who waits for us.

When we do that, life becomes a teachable moment. Then we become open to seeing even the painful moments transformed into moments of laughter. Then we can grow and know what it is for the Spirit to descend on us, and for our hearts to be open to God's new dream coming, and we will hear the voice of our heavenly Father speaking over us: 'This is my child, whom I love. With her/him I am well pleased!'

Questions for Reflection

1. Where does your patience run thin? For me, the driver was fear. Do you know what drives your impatience?

2. Several strategies were outlined in this chapter to help us resist society's pressures. Which strategy challenges you most? Is it:
   a. saving for something rather than always having it now;
   b. disengaging from the 24/7 information cycle;
   c. using 'dead time' as an opportunity, not a loss?

3. The Bible gives plenty of examples of people who had to wait, including David. How might God be using the 'waiting time' to develop you?

4. What hopes might we need to let go of, handing them over to God's care?

5. How does the idea that God chooses to wait help you wait?

6. If you drew a timeline of your life and significant events so far, what would you see?

Finding Common Ground

A lot has happened to David in our journey so far. He has been on a remarkable journey.

From the unknown shepherd boy of Bethlehem to giant-slayer.

From the son-in-law of King Saul to fugitive and enemy of the state.

David has been on the run, and then he goes and lives among the Philistines, the historical enemy of God's people, whom he defeated many times in battle. It is hard to find a comparison for this decision that fits into our modern, western culture.

As a Spurs fan, the closest I can come to comparing David's actions would be for me to buy a season ticket to go and watch Arsenal. That would be pretty bad! In fact it's unthinkable! But what David did was even worse than that – just. He went to live with the mortal enemy of his own people, and during that time, Saul, and David's best friend Jonathan, Saul's son, were killed in a battle with the Philistines. Israel was defeated.

David was anointed as king over Judah – the southern kingdom – but is now at war with the northern kingdom, Israel, which is still loyal to Saul's family. Saul's supporters are defeated by David, and so we come to this passage, where David unites the kingdoms as one nation:

> All the tribes of Israel came to David at Hebron and said, 'We are your own flesh and blood. In the past, while Saul was king over us, you were the one who led Israel on their military campaigns. And the LORD said to you, "You shall shepherd my people Israel, and you shall become their ruler."'
>
> When all the elders of Israel had come to King David at Hebron, the king made a covenant with them at Hebron before the LORD, and they anointed David king over Israel.
>
> David was thirty years old when he became king, and he reigned for forty years. In Hebron he reigned over Judah for seven years and six months, and in Jerusalem he reigned over all Israel and Judah for thirty-three years.[1]

So David becomes king, but he is immediately faced with a challenge. How to unify these two former enemies and establish them as one kingdom?

Common Ground

A couple of chapters ago we looked at conflict and how there are times within conflict when you might need to compromise. Common ground is different from compromise. It goes deeper.

There are times when compromise can be easier to achieve than common ground because compromise is a mechanism for de-escalating conflict, whereas common ground is a place to stand with someone.

Think about the conflicts or disagreements that have taken place in your life. It may be that, in some of these cases, you agreed to compromise in order to bring the conflict to an end, and that was a really important thing you were willing to do; but what about the prospect of standing by that person in unity? In the moment, that doesn't really seem possible.

I was talking recently with a man – I'll call him Jim – who attends one of the local AA groups here in Bath. He has been sober for over fifty years and was speaking to me about his friendship with another man who had also racked up an impressive number of years of sobriety and, in fact, had been sober for six months longer than Jim had. Jim told me that he hadn't initially warmed to this man when they first met; to be honest, he really didn't like him. They came from different backgrounds. Jim came from a poor family, had been involved in gang life and had recently come out of prison after serving eight years of a twelve-year sentence for stabbing a policeman. His friend, however, was from a wealthy background, had played rugby professionally and was a very different character. These two men were from different worlds, with different personalities. They were unlikely friends, but nonetheless they became friends, and stayed friends for fifty years. Now they are close because, despite all their differences, they found common ground in the illness that they had in common and in their commitment to battle it together one day at a time.

Common ground is possible, even in the most unlikely of places. We'll come back to Jim a little bit later.

At the start of 2 Samuel 5 we read that David has now become king of both Judah and Israel, two neighbouring tribal kingdoms. He had reigned as king over Judah alone for seven and a half years, and then at the age of 30 he unites the kingdoms of Israel and Judah together as he becomes king of Israel.

How was he going to bring people together? How was he going to heal the divisions that had occurred and take them forward as a united nation? It was no small task, and as the saying goes, now that the war was won it was time to win the peace.

For these two tribal neighbours, their common ground would not be found primarily in a place but in a person. David himself was their common ground, a king over both kingdoms, the one who brought them together. This is what the Israelite delegation came to say to him: 'You are the one. You are God's chosen one to lead us, and so the common ground we now share with Judah is a king whom God has chosen.' And in that sense, their coming together, their stepping on to common ground together, was stepping into the purposes of God.

After all, it was David who had been anointed by Samuel, it was David on whom the Spirit of God rested, and it was David who could unite this people.

How often is it that we find common ground in a person? This might be a friend or a family member.

Israel and Judah shared common ground in David; but David was determined to take them deeper, to take them to new ground – to ensure that they had a future together too.

New Ground

David now faces an interesting and important decision. Where to have his capital city? While he was king in Judah, his capital had been Hebron, but that was unlikely to be acceptable to Israel. Equally, if he moved his capital deep into Israel, it was likely to be seen by Judah as rejection. There would have been people pressing him from both sides to pick their territory. There would have been those from Judah who were saying, 'The capital has to be here in Judah'; and there would have been those from Israel who were saying, 'The capital has to be here in Israel.'

So David does something shrewd:

> The king and his men marched to Jerusalem to attack the Jebusites, who lived there. The Jebusites said to David, 'You will not get in here; even the blind and the lame can ward you off.' They thought, 'David cannot get in here.' Nevertheless, David captured the fortress of Zion – which is the City of David.
>
> On that day David had said, 'Anyone who conquers the Jebusites will have to use the water shaft to reach those "lame and blind" who are David's enemies.' That is why they say, 'The "blind and lame" will not enter the palace.'
>
> David then took up residence in the fortress and called it the City of David. He built up the area around it, from the terraces inwards. And he became more and more powerful, because the LORD God Almighty was with him.[2]

David targets the Jebusite stronghold of Jerusalem, a territory within the borders of Israel but not part of its tribal lands or systems. Neither was it part of Judah.

David had come across a tricky situation, a sensitive situation that was going to mark his kingship, so he decided to do something new. He wanted not only to be a place of common ground but also to take the people into new ground – ground where no one had a claim, but because of that, everyone could claim it as their own.

Jerusalem was new ground for David, and it was Jerusalem that David set his sights on as the new capital.

This is what the Americans did when they were trying to find a new capital for their newly independent United States. They chose the one place which was not linked to any of the existing states: the District of Columbia, and its main city: Washington. No state could thus lay claim to the capital, and because of that it was a place which all could claim as theirs. It was new ground for all.

And that new capital for Judah and Israel was more than just new ground for them physically, a new place for them to call home at the centre of the newly united nation. It was a new identity for them as well, because David did something different with the name of the city.

I had often thought that David renamed the city from 'Jebus' (the Jebusite name) to 'Jerusalem', but in fact the link between the two names goes back beyond David. The first mention we have of Jerusalem is in Joshua 10:1, where we read about Adoni-Zedek, the 'king of Jerusalem'.

Later we see the link between the two names in Judges 19:10: 'But, unwilling to stay another night, the man left and went towards Jebus (that is, Jerusalem), with his two saddled donkeys and his concubine.'

So perhaps the city's name wasn't totally changed, but it was redeemed. The Jebusite meaning of the name Jerusalem meant 'the foundation of Salem', who was one of their gods.

However, the meaning of Jerusalem in Hebrew is 'rain of peace'. The meaning of the verb *yara*, at the start of the word *Jeru*-salem, is to do with bringing lots of different smaller things together in a single effect; for example, raindrops are single drops of water but when they come together they have the single effect of rain. The ending of the name Jeru-*salem* is the word *shalem*, which means wholeness or completeness. We know it best as *shalom*: peace.

This may have been the redeeming of the name Jerusalem. It no longer meant the foundation of a city devoted to a foreign god. Now, for the Hebrew people, it was the city of the 'rain of peace' – the place where God would bring together these individual people into a single effect, to be the means of his peace, his wholeness and completeness to the nations.

It was not simply new ground in terms of geography; it was also a new identity, rich in the meaning of all that God was bringing about.

So what about us? Where is our common ground and our new ground?

What do you do when you have two groups with a difficult history, each thinking that they have a claim to the future? You find common ground, and new ground.

Our Common Ground

Think about any dispute between two sides. Perhaps think about times when a dispute like that has happened in your own life. Often, one of the challenges we face is that we think we are right. We feel we have right on our side, sometimes even that we have God on our side. We therefore think that we are owed a certain future, where our way of thinking, our view, is the one that comes out on top. Sometimes we are unwilling to see things from the other side's point of view. Sometimes we are unwilling to listen. Sometimes we are unwilling to find common ground. Like Jim and his friend from

AA whom we met earlier on, it might seem as though you are worlds apart and there is nothing that you have in common.

Whether it is the most entrenched religious divide that sees nations go to war with nations, or a dispute between two friends, or a disagreement within a church; more often than not, when we take the time to reflect upon it, there is common ground that we can step into together.

1. There is common ground in our humanity

Whatever faith we come from, or nationality we hold to, the one thing that we all have in common is our humanity.

Over the centuries, this is what people have sought to express in the great political declarations that form new nations or new movements. In eighteenth-century France, in a nation made up of people from different social, economic and political backgrounds, what could the leaders say to find common ground after the French Revolution? 'Men are born and remain free and *equal* in rights. Social distinctions can be founded only in the common good.'[3]

Or what about the United States of America? Having thrown off the rule of Great Britain during the War of Independence, and thinking about who they wanted to be as a newly formed nation, what common ground could the Americans find? 'We hold these truths to be self-evident, that all men are created *equal*, and endowed by their creator with certain unalienable Rights, that among these are Life, Liberty and the pursuit of Happiness.'[4]

Or read this statement several centuries later when, following the horrors of two world wars in less than forty years, the world came together to build, out of the rubble, the United Nations: 'All human beings are born free and *equal* in dignity and rights. They are endowed with reason and conscience and should act towards one another in a spirit of brotherhood.'[5]

All these major works speak about the equality of human beings, that is, the common ground that we share, no matter what our other differences might be.

But what do we mean when we say that? Is this simply a matter of biology? Is it a case of stripping away all our differences until we find unity in our uniformity?

For me it is, and has to be, more than that.

Let's go back to the very beginning;

> So God created mankind in his own image,
>   in the image of God he created them;
>   male and female he created them.[6]

We are created, each one of us, by God and in the image of God. We each share that. No matter what our differences, no matter how we may look at another person and see something that is 'other' than us, this is the one thing that we cannot remove, even if we fail to see it.

Our humanity is like a giant canvas on which the human story has been painted. Different parts of a famous work of art will look different, with different colours and paints and brush strokes, but it is on one canvas that this masterpiece is painted. It's a bit like that with our humanity. We are different shapes, different colours; we move in different ways; but the thing that brings us together, the common ground on which we stand, is found most easily in our shared humanity – in the fact that each of us is created by a God who loves us; in the fact that each person, no matter his or her colour or shape or movement, is created in the image of God.

It is easier to see that common ground when the person stepping on to it with you happens to look like you, or think like you, or believe what you do. Sometimes the common ground we share goes beyond skin-deep, or transcends our creeds and allegiances. Sometimes we have to work to find it beneath the surface. But we can do it with a recognition of our humanity, with the belief that each of us contains within our DNA the fingerprints of the Maker's touch, and that every single one of us breathes because the Creator's breath still infuses the very fibres of our being.

If we believe this, if we look for this in one another, then perhaps this can change the way we see and *what* we see: those who have different views from us, or who look different from us, or who live in a way that we do not agree with. Suddenly, there is more that we share as human beings than we first thought.

2. For the church, the common ground is Jesus

The Son is the image of the invisible God, the firstborn over all creation. For in him all things were created: things in heaven and on earth, visible and invisible, whether thrones or powers or rulers or authorities; all things have been created through him and for him. He is before all things, and *in him all things hold together*. And he is the head of the body, the church; he is the beginning and the firstborn from among the dead, so that in everything he might have the supremacy.[7]

'In him all things hold together.' Jesus is our common ground.

That might seem simplistic, but it is the truth engraved through the whole identity of the church and it is a truth that we need to remind ourselves of constantly, because we have a tendency to wander off and try to find our identity or common ground in other things. As the church, it is easy for us to think that our common ground is what we believe, the creeds we recite or the statements of faith we say yes to. But the problem with those things is that they change. The church has been debating for years what those things should be, and even when we do share a creed or statement of faith, there are often different focuses between various churches. Think about your own church for a moment. It is fairly likely that over the years, your church's leaders have changed their minds on any number of 'key issues'.

Of course it is important to know what we believe, and wherever that means we can reach out to others then that's a great thing, but surely for our common ground to be secure it needs to be set upon something a little more stable than the changing doctrine of the church.

It needs to be personal – just as it was for the people of Judah and Israel all those years ago. For them, their unity was not in some common statement of faith, or shared goals. It was in a king. And for us, our common ground is in King Jesus, the one who brings us together, the one under whom we come together. He is the head of the church.

It is important to keep the distinction between what we believe about Jesus, and Jesus himself. When we say that the common ground we share as the church is Jesus, what we often actually mean is what we believe about Jesus. Then we come back to creeds. But as I have said, this is personal. It requires me to walk in relationship with the living Lord Jesus, and for you to walk in relationship with the living Lord Jesus, and then, no matter what other differences we have, we have solid common ground.

That common ground, found in relationship with God as Father, Son and Holy Spirit, is expressed powerfully by Paul in Ephesians 4:

> As a prisoner for the Lord, then, I urge you to live a life worthy of the calling you have received. Be completely humble and gentle; be patient, bearing with one another in love. Make every effort to keep the unity of the Spirit through the bond of peace. There is one body and *one Spirit*, just as you were called to one hope when you were called; *one Lord*, one faith, one baptism; *one God and Father* of all, who is over all and through all and in all.[8]

As we step on to that common ground, then, like the people of God coming together all those years ago, we step into the purposes of God for us as well. This is because in Christ we are made to come together, which is at the heart of the prayer that Jesus prayed in John 17. Having prayed for his disciples, he prays for us: 'My prayer is not for them alone. I pray also for those who will believe in me through their message, that all of them may be one, Father, just as you are in me and I am in you. May they also be in us so that the world may believe that you have sent me.'[9]

If we want to make a difference in the world, to be a missional people who show society that we are Jesus' followers through the way we love one another, then it starts as we root ourselves in Jesus. When we step together on to that common ground of knowing a common Saviour and Friend, then it's not simply about ticking some creedal box. It's about experiencing, in a real but mysterious way, how all that we have been, all we are and all we ever hope to be is drawn together in him.

Then we can celebrate one another's successes and find comfort in one another's struggles, because as we step on to common ground we have a vested interest in one another. Then we can look at others – other believers or other churches – who are doing well and we can be blessed, because that success builds up the whole body. That, I am sure, was the case for the newly united kingdom under David, and when we are united together it is the reality for the church as well.

The call throughout Scripture is to live in unity. In the Psalms we read:

How good and pleasant it is
when God's people live together in unity![10]

The psalmist goes on to say that it is here, in this unity, that God commands a blessing.

But we must not confuse unity with uniformity. As individuals, we do not all need to look the same, and neither do our communities. God has created you uniquely, and the only image that he wants you to strive to conform to is that of Jesus. His desire is that you, the unique and precious you that he has made, will look more and more like Jesus as you follow him. You do not need to look like your worship leader, your pastor, your youth leader, your small-group leader, your parents or anyone else. There is room within unity for diversity, but uniformity kills unity because it fails to value the 'other' unless it looks the same.

Our New Ground

What are the strongholds in your life? Do those strongholds mean that it is harder for you to step on to common ground with others?

One of the strongholds for both Israel and Judah would have been their tribal identities. There wasn't anything wrong with those identities, but this was a moment for coming together rather than remaining divided.

Sometimes the strongholds in our lives require us to let go of things in order to reach common ground, but that can be a challenge for us. There are strongholds in our culture as well as the strongholds in our theology, and both can be a barrier to stepping on to common ground.

Think about what happens when there is a debate about making changes within the life of a church, something I have had my fair share of over the years. There are challenges we face at such times because, whether you are on the side of change or the side of keeping things as they are, strongholds are those places where we say: 'It has to be here' or 'It has to be like this.'

At the time of writing, the Church of England is about to embark on a consultation about same-sex marriage. This is not the place for a discussion about that particular issue, but the process does highlight the difficulty of coming to common ground when we have strongholds in our lives. I was on a walk recently with a friend who is an Anglican vicar, and we were talking about that consultation in the light of my writing this chapter. On either side of the debate there are those who have strong views on the rights and wrongs of their position and of the other side's position. My friend told me that both sides were already 'setting up camp and getting it ready' as the discussion came ever closer.

I said to my friend that those entrenched views are unlikely to shift. Ten per cent of people at either end of the spectrum have made up their minds, and their only engagement in the process is to argue their corner. They are not listening to hear; rather, they are listening to respond.

My friend pointed out to me that even when those strong views exist, it is still important to be able to come together and listen, to be open, to sit at the table. We need to take a position not always as the *host* but as the *guest*. It may be that sitting at the table of the person whose views are the opposite to your own is new ground for you, but it may be a significant and strategic action in the quest to find common ground.

I think it is worth reflecting that there is a difference between a strong view and a stronghold. We can have strong views about things, things we hold to and believe deeply, that don't become strongholds. When they become strongholds it is because we have put up walls, and we hide behind them, throwing pitch and mortar down on those who get too close.

As we think about what those strongholds might be for us, and as we acknowledge that their presence makes finding common ground more difficult, the important thing to see from our Scripture passage is that the people of this newly united nation under David did not move to new ground on their own. They were *led* to new ground. David took them to new ground.

It is the same for us too. We do not move to new ground on our own, but Jesus can take us to new ground. In fact, Jesus does take us to new ground. But very often that new ground means we have to let go of what we had before, the strongholds we have based ourselves in, and take hold of something different – something new. We don't like the idea of new ground sometimes. We think to ourselves, *I want to stick with what I know, with what is familiar, with what feels right.*

In the previous chapter, we looked at how God calls us to 'let go' of control, and to know that he is God. In this area of finding common ground, as with our times of waiting, are there things that God is asking you to let go of, to relax your grip of? Is he asking you to trust him to be God?

No matter what side of the fence we are on, what camp we find ourselves in, perhaps we can be a little bit like the people of Judah and Israel when they were thinking about their capital. Maybe we too say, 'It has to be here,' more often than we should, and the 'here' might look different for each of us. It might be that some are saying, 'It has to be open' or 'It has to be closed'; 'It has to be progressive' or 'It has to be traditional'; 'It has to change' or 'It has to stay the same.' I wonder, are those familiar phrases in your life, or in the life of your church?

So, what is the new ground for us? In many ways that isn't always clear, but what we do know, or rather *who* we know, is all that matters.

All that matters – *all* that matters – is that this is the church of Jesus. Jesus is the head of the church, and the call that he offered to those first disciples is the call that he offers to you and me each and every day: 'Follow me.' Perhaps we are so used to singing our songs of worship to Jesus that we have forgotten to actually follow him; we have become so used to asking him to bless our plans that we have forgotten to listen to his. We are the followers, and he is the one we follow.

And in the future he might call us to stand on new ground. So we need to be awake and looking for the new thing that he might be doing, for the new place he might be leading us to. After all, this is a God who says in Isaiah 43:

Forget the former things;
> do not dwell on the past.
See, I am doing a new thing![11]

Whatever the strongholds are for us, wherever we find we have settled and don't want to move from, King Jesus is calling us forward on to common ground, new ground. And with that comes a new identity. Jerusalem became a place where all the nations of the world came to worship. It became a place of welcome, a place of inclusion, a shining city on a hill. It was the place where God lived in his temple; the place where Jesus died and rose again to save us; the place where the Holy Spirit breathed life on a fledgling church.

I can't tell you what the new ground will look like. I'm not the King. More often than I would like, I am the one saying, 'It has to be like this . . . ' But what I *can* tell you is that when Jesus calls us to new ground, when we step on to it, he will build something that will be a light to all the peoples, a shining city on the hill of our lives and our life together, where God himself will live and breathe life into our fragile places. It will be a new Jerusalem, built not with stones but with the lives of all who would respond to his call to follow him, and be saturated by his rain of peace. This is the city of the God who says, 'See, I am making all things new.'[12]

Questions for Reflection

1. Can you think of any obstacles to your finding common ground with others? Do these prevent you from being able to move to new ground?

2. How is finding common ground different from compromise?

3. For Israel and Judah, their common ground was David. Can you think of any other examples, either from the Bible or life in general, where people united around a person?

4. How do we understand our common ground in relation to:
   a. our humanity;
   b. our Jesus?

5. Why is unity not the same as uniformity?

6. What might you have to let go of in order to step on to the common ground Jesus is calling you to? Why is it important that we hold on to Jesus as we follow this path?

6

Mephibosheth

I don't know what you remember of the story of Mephibosheth, but it is a story full of depth and emotion. It brings together the themes of grace, covenant love and friendship, and speaks to us today about how we too can be people who reflect God's heart in our relationships with others.

My son Leo is 5 years old as I write, and so it's difficult to think of the story of Mephibosheth without thinking about him. When Mephibosheth was just 5 years old, tragedy struck his family. Living in the palace at Gibeon, the peace and protection of this place and his family name was suddenly ripped away as word came that his grandfather Saul, king of Israel, and his father Jonathan, Saul's heir, had been killed in battle with the Philistines.

Panic gripped the palace as the royal household faced two immediate risks, first from the Philistines themselves, and second, from David. With Saul and Jonathan gone, surely David would look to seize the throne and at the same time remove any potential challenge to his rule. This was what kings did when they came to power.

The only thing to do was to run – to head for the ancestral and tribal lands where at least there would be some protection.

Amid all that panic, amid all the noise and confusion, with people running through the corridors to gather possessions to take on the road, a young nurse carries a small boy. As she fights her way through the commotion, trying not to panic the child, trying to calm him, the unthinkable happens. Perhaps she slips; maybe she is knocked; but the result is that the young child slips from her grasp and falls to the ground. Screams of pain interrupt the chaos all around as she realizes that he is seriously injured. What she doesn't know is that the fall has shattered his tiny bones. But there is no time to cry, no time to rest, no time to heal. Now they must run, so she picks up the screaming child again and they escape into hiding.

Those little bones would never set straight, and Mephibosheth would always struggle to walk.

There is more to the story, which we will track as we continue through the chapter, but you can read the full account of it in 2 Samuel 9.

Grace Is Costly

David asked, 'Is there anyone still left of the house of Saul to whom I can show kindness for Jonathan's sake?'

Now there was a servant of Saul's household named Ziba. They summoned him to appear before David, and the king said to him, 'Are you Ziba?'

'At your service,' he replied.

The king asked, 'Is there no one still alive from the house of Saul to whom I can show God's kindness?'

Ziba answered the king, 'There is still a son of Jonathan; he is lame in both feet.'[1]

It is easy to be kind to a friend. It is easy to be kind to someone who has been kind to you, even if you don't know that person. But what about a total stranger you have just met?

What about a person who is a threat to you?

This was the position that David found himself in. Mephibosheth was a rival to David because he came from the former royal house. That's why he had been in hiding all those years.

It's important for us to understand the context, and to realize what usually happened to the former royal line when a new king came to town, because it highlights that what David does is not only countercultural but also costly.

It's easier to show grace to people when it costs us nothing to show that grace. But what about the times when there is a cost? What about the occasions when there is a risk?

So, what was the risk here?

Mephibosheth, as we read in 2 Samuel 9:1, is from the house of Saul. The house of David and the house of Saul had historically been at war. We have already seen earlier in the book how the relationship between Saul and David had broken down, and how Saul had hunted David and chased him all round the country.

When Saul died, there was a struggle for the throne. Saul's son Ish-Bosheth became king over Israel, and David became king over Judah. In 2 Samuel 3 we read that 'the war between the house of Saul and the house of David lasted a long time'.[2]

This state of hostility between David and the house of Saul lasted for several years. There was pain and tension, and resentment towards David when he became king.

But what does David try to do? He does not attempt to get even or remove the threat, but to show kindness.

The word 'kindness' used here is a translation of the Hebrew word *hesed*. This goes far deeper than just a simple or one-off act of kindness. It is far more than simply 'being nice'. It is long-lasting faithful love that is rooted in relationship. Eugene Peterson says that *hesed* is 'love without regard to shifting circumstances, hormones, emotional states, and personal convenience'.[3]

It is costly to love those close to us with that kind of love, because it requires something of us – a piece of our hearts, a slice of our souls. It is the giving of who we are, rather than simply our affection. This is why it is often called 'covenant love', a deep binding together that has been used to describe the love between a husband and a wife; and even the love between God and human beings.

This is the love that David wants to show to Mephibosheth. The reason why David would want to do this is because he himself has been a recipient of it. He has experienced it, been touched by it, and had given it in return – to Mephibosheth's father, Jonathan.

In many ways, David's relationship with Jonathan was *the* defining relationship at the defining time in David's life.

So often, this is true in our own lives too. When we have received grace in the context of a loving relationship, we are more likely to pass it on to others. When we have freely received, we can also freely give. Perhaps you have experienced that in relationships in the past? Whether or not we can answer 'yes' to this question when thinking about our human relationships, as Christians we can all affirm that we have received this from God.

God's love for us is mirrored in the story of David and Mephibosheth. Like David seeking Mephibosheth, so God seeks us out in love. The catalyst for this search is nothing other than deep, abiding, covenant love. A love that breaks down all barriers, turns over every stone and, like a raging fire, cannot be quenched. Just as Paul said to the Romans: 'I am convinced that neither death nor life, neither angels nor demons, neither the present nor the future, nor any powers, neither height nor depth, nor anything else in all creation, will be able to separate us from the love of God that is in Christ Jesus our Lord.'[4]

The similarity doesn't stop there. Outside of David's relationship with Jonathan, Mephibosheth deserved nothing from David. As we have seen, his very existence was problematic for David. This was grace at its most wonderful and dynamic, breaking down the notion that love, favour and compassion have to be earned. Rather, grace is a gift to be received joyously and unexpectedly; but it is always drawing us in to relationship. We will explore more of this later in the chapter.

David doesn't wait for Mephibosheth to come looking or begging. His love reaches out not just to someone who is indifferent but to someone who is hostile. As we read in the first letter of John: 'This is love: not that we loved God, but that he loved us and sent his Son as an atoning sacrifice for our sins.'[5]

Once again, we see here a mirror of God's grace to us. God doesn't wait for us to be ready, to come begging; he comes. He leaves the ninety-nine sheep in search of the missing one; he turns the house upside down in search of the lost coin; he searches the horizon for the wayward child and then runs to meet them. God does not wait for us to love him; his love is bigger than that.

So what life lesson can we learn here? If we have been recipients of this kind of grace, this kind of love, then surely we must pass it on to others. Otherwise, have we really received it, been changed and affected by it? That is John's very argument in 1 John 4:11: 'Dear friends, since God so loved us, we also ought to love one another.'

In the same way that Jonathan's love shapes and changes David, but also compels him to reach out to others, even the least deserving, so the love that we have received from God should shape and change us, and compel us to reach out in love to those around us, even the least deserving.

Grace Reaches into Those Hard-to-Reach Places

'Where is he?' the king asked.

Ziba answered, 'He is at the house of Makir son of Ammiel in Lo Debar.'[6]

When we hear of Mephibosheth, he is living in Lo Debar, a small place with a significant name. The Hebrew word *lo* means 'no', and the word *debar* means 'pasture' or 'word'. Mephibosheth is living in the place of no pasture, or the place of no word. It is the forgotten place, the middle of nowhere. It is a place you go to because you don't want to remember or be remembered. As R.T. Kendall says of Mephibosheth: 'He thought he was of no account and that everyone had forgotten about him.'[7] Have you ever felt like that? That you aren't worth anything or that you seem to have slipped off the radar? Perhaps that's a choice you have made to cope with the pains and the challenges of life.

This is a common experience, and at times it appears to be a straightforward choice to make in response to pain: to head for Lo Debar. After all, how can someone hurt me when I am not around?

There will be times when that kind of choice is needed and is healing, but there are two things I want to say about Lo Debar as we reflect on it in the context of this story.

First, the place itself was not as significant as what was going on inside Mephibosheth. There was the physical place he went to in order to escape; and then there was the inner world of his heart and mind in which he became a prisoner – a prisoner to shame, to bitterness, to self-hatred. If you wonder how we can know what's going on inside his heart and mind during this time, then we just have to jump ahead a little in the story and see how Mephibosheth describes himself when he comes face to face with David: 'What is your servant, that you should notice a dead dog like me?'[8]

We may choose to physically take ourselves away from pain and hurt, but we take ourselves with us wherever we go, and it can sometimes be the case that we enter an internal state of Lo Debar where we too are imprisoned by our pain, shame and bitterness. In this state, our self-worth can plummet, and we can find ourselves thinking, when faced with the prospect of other relationships, *What would they want with a dead dog like me?*

There are lots of events that can lead us into our Lo Debars.

Perhaps you lost someone close to you? It can seem safer to distance yourself from others because of the fear of losing another person who is close to you.

Perhaps it was fear of the way others looked at you? You end up viewing yourself as less than others and distance yourself from them in order to protect yourself from more pain and rejection.

Perhaps you were dropped by someone who was meant to carry you? For Mephibosheth, it was his nurse. For you, it might be a parent who was meant to care for you but abandoned you. Or a spouse who was meant to be faithful to you but left you. Or a safe person who was meant to protect you but abused you. The consequences of being dropped by others can leave us with permanent injury, meaning we may never walk the same way again.

Mephibosheth was helpless in Lo Debar. He couldn't do anything to change his situation. He wasn't living; he was surviving – getting through another day in the hopes that there wouldn't be *that* knock at the door. That helplessness led to hopelessness. He felt that he was not only helpless in that moment, but would always be helpless, a prisoner to this situation and his own pain; hope seemed to have evaporated like moisture from the hot desert sand.

Are there moments when you feel like this too? That not only is there pain in your current situation but you also cannot see how anything is ever going to change. Your helplessness gives way to hopelessness.

It's worth noting, too, that Mephibosheth has been wrestling with these issues since he was a child. As a small boy of 5, he lost his father and life as he knew it. His childhood disappeared before his very eyes in a 1-metre fall. These feelings of hopelessness, of despair, shame and hatred, were not passing moods. They were deep-seated from childhood.

In a couple of my previous books I have mentioned that when I was 3 years old my dad died unexpectedly of a stroke at the age of 34. My life changed forever at that moment. While I had the joy of a new stepdad when my mum remarried several years later, in many ways the major journey of my life has been to process that early loss. It is really only now, at an older age than my father was when he died, and with a young son of my own, that I am consciously working through my feelings surrounding his death. My point in sharing that is simply this: what happens to us when we are young can profoundly shape us for the rest of our lives. John Powell highlights this for us in his book *Why Am I Afraid to Love?* He writes: 'Although it is difficult to accept, the psychological scars that we have acquired during the first seven years remain in some way with us for life.'[9]

That might be the case for you. It might be that you are struggling with something that was set into your very foundations at a young age; something that you are struggling to walk with even many years later. Mephibosheth, despite his acceptance from David, always struggled to walk. Some scars do not heal easily, and some we carry with us for our whole lives.

Lo Debar is a horrible place. It is a place you would not choose to visit, but for many it is a place they call home. Not because they want to, but because for one reason or another this is where they have found themselves. There is a painful irony here: they have chosen to graze in the place of no pasture.

I think of the homeless people who sit on the step of our church. They are passed by, every single day, by people who refuse not only to talk to them but often even to look at them. They are asked to move on across the city, sometimes when it's necessary, but more often because in a beautiful city like Bath it 'doesn't look good'. They sit in plain sight, yet they live in a place of forgotten-ness, of no pasture. It may be that they have wandered into that place themselves, or due to events that have happened to them. However, even in our most gracious moments as a society, we often fail to help them out, and at our worst we actively contribute to keeping them there, constantly moving them out of sight so that they can be out of mind.

For some, Lo Debar is wherever they go.

However, there is good news to be found even in Lo Debar.

Grace can reach into even the hardest-to-reach places. There is no expectation in Lo Debar. As I said a moment ago, it is a place of hopelessness. If we look at the names in this Scripture passage, we see that clearly. Mephibosheth, whose name means 'shame', is living in Lo Debar, which means 'no word' or 'no pasture', in the house of Makir, whose name means 'slave'. Everything about Mephibosheth in this moment seems hopeless, and yet what this story shows us is that even here, good news can come. Even here, grace can break in.

It reminds me of another story in the Old Testament, the story of Hagar in Genesis 16:

> The angel of the Lord found Hagar near a spring in the desert; it was the spring that is beside the road to Shur. And he said, 'Hagar, slave of Sarai, where have you come from, and where are you going?'
>
> 'I'm running away from my mistress Sarai,' she answered.
>
> Then the angel of the Lord told her, 'Go back to your mistress and submit to her.' The angel added, 'I will increase your descendants so much that they will be too numerous to count.' . . .
>
> She gave this name to the Lord who spoke to her: 'You are the God who sees me,' for she said, 'I have now seen the One who sees me.'[10]

Hagar suffered immensely at the hands of a family who really were meant to carry her. In the end, the constant bullying and abuse are too much for her and she runs into the desert. For a pregnant woman to risk the brutally harsh conditions of the desert gives you an indication of just how bad things had become, but here in the desert she has an unexpected encounter. She meets God. Whether the person she meets is a divine messenger or in some form God himself, Hagar is in no doubt that she has met God. And she is given a rare privilege that few in the Bible are given. She gets to give God a name, and the name that she chooses is El-Roi: 'the God who sees me'. What a beautiful name it is! It speaks of her amazement that she, an outcast female slave on the run from an abusive family, should be noticed by God. The fact that he notices her and cares for her, calling her by name even as she wanders through the Negev desert, should give us reason to hope that no matter how isolated, lost and hidden we feel, our God is El-Roi, the God who sees us. We may feel as if that phrase should have two words added to it: '. . . even here'. He is the God who sees me *even here*. Because you might expect to be seen in the first family of the people of God; you might expect to be seen in the palace of a king, or in your church or your family. But when you are in a place where you have been dropped or abused, and you have fled into the wilderness or into Lo Debar, it seems as though any hope that someone might see you or notice you has gone. But even here, God sees you. He sees your brokenness and pain; he sees your shame and hurt; he sees all that's underneath that too. All the wonder and the beauty, the goodness and trust he also sees, because he sees the 'you' that perhaps you have forgotten how to see; the you that you are afraid to dare to hope is still there.

And God sees you with the eyes of a father, with the eyes of a protector. There is no place, whether it is the Negev desert, or Lo Debar, or the scenes of your forgotten-ness, where you escape his loving gaze. As David himself prays in Psalm 139:

> Where can I go from your Spirit?
> > Where can I flee from your presence?
> If I go up to the heavens, you are there;
> > if I make my bed in the depths, you are there.
> If I rise on the wings of the dawn,
> > if I settle on the far side of the sea,
> even there your hand will guide me,
> > your right hand will hold me fast.
> If I say, 'Surely the darkness will hide me
> > and the light become night around me,'
> even the darkness will not be dark to you;
> > the night will shine like the day,
> > for darkness is as light to you.[11]

Even here, in Lo Debar, Mephibosheth is not beyond the tender gaze of God's grace.

As we will go on to see in this story, God in his grace doesn't leave us in Lo Debar either.

Grace Restores Us

There are several things that we see in this encounter between David and Mephiboseth which are worth pausing to reflect upon as we seek to learn lessons for our own lives.

Before we get there, can you imagine for a moment the scene in David's throne room? All the courtiers, advisers, guards and family members standing around the king. The splendour of the palace. Suddenly the doors open and a broken figure struggles in. Every step is painful to take; every glance from others is painful to receive. Then this disabled man prostrates himself before the king – an action which would have caused a great deal of pain.

David breaks this tension with one word. A name – Mephibosheth: 'When Mephibosheth son of Jonathan, the son of Saul, came to David, he bowed down to pay him honour. David said, "Mephibosheth!"'[12] That's the first thing that draws our attention.

1. David says Mephibosheth's name

Names are significant, as we have already seen in this chapter. Mephibosheth means 'shame'. But the king doesn't say his name in order to highlight his shame, but rather to acknowledge him. Remember that he has come from Lo Debar, the place of no name, and the first thing he hears from David is his name. How often must he have tried to keep that name a secret over the years? When anyone sympathetic to David came into the area, his survival depended on that name being kept a secret. But here he was, before the very king he had been hiding from, and he hears his name.

It reminds me again of the story of Hagar, but it also reminds me of the story of Mary Magdalene in the garden when she meets the resurrected Jesus, who simply calls her by name: 'Mary.'[13]

It is a way of saying, 'I see you.'

How often do we need that in our lives? When we have been living in the place of forgotten-ness, of no name, how wonderful it is for someone to say 'I see you'. You are worth mentioning; you are worth noticing. In those places of Lo Debar our identity is stripped away. We fear the people we are and we fear what will happen if people find out who we are. What will happen if people see the real me? Will I be met with judgement, or acceptance? Because we fear judgement and condemnation we stay hidden away, out of sight. Perhaps you have been brave enough to show who you are to others before, but you have been rejected. Maybe you find it hard to trust that this time it could be different.

However you have been received by others, you can always be yourself, your true and authentic self, before God. In one of my favourite verses in the Bible, God simply says this:

> But now, this is what the LORD says –
>> he who created you, Jacob,
>> he who formed you, Israel:
> 'Do not fear, for I have redeemed you;
>> I have summoned you by name; you are mine.'[14]

He sees us completely, and he knows who we are – the real us, the us that at times we keep hidden from others because we feel ashamed or afraid. God is not a search party come to hunt you down and condemn you, but a loving Father who longs to speak these words over your life. So why not read that verse from Isaiah to yourself today, but replace the names 'Jacob' and 'Israel' with your own name.

Step one to being restored is to allow yourself to be seen. As you grow in confidence as one who is seen and noticed by the almighty one of heaven, perhaps you will grow in confidence to allow others to see you too.

2. David calms Mephibosheth's fears

The second thing that we notice in this passage is that David says: 'Don't be afraid . . .'[15]

As we have already seen in this chapter, in his mind Mephibosheth had every reason to be afraid. Knowing the war that had raged between David and the house of Saul, as well as the custom that the incoming king would kill the successor from a rival house to prevent them from becoming a threat, perhaps he had good reason to be afraid. Eugene Peterson reflects on that journey: 'Every step brought him nearer to his anticipated doom. The wretched tale of his victimised life would terminate now in bloody execution.'[16]

With all this fear I am sure that the one thing Mephibosheth wasn't expecting was to have his fears calmed. To hear these words, 'Do not be afraid,' spoken by the king, the one who had the power to condemn him, must have been a shock.

Once again, for us, as we fear our past and what that will mean as we come into the presence of the King, we too are met with a surprise. The one who could condemn us chooses not to. Our fears, with him, are unfounded. He says to us: 'Do not be afraid.'

Paul, when writing to the early church in Rome, reminds them of something powerful which we too need to hear as we approach the King: 'There is now no condemnation for those who are in Christ Jesus.'[17]

Why shouldn't Mephibosheth be afraid? The reason is his father. It is because of the love between David and Jonathan that Mephibosheth has no reason to fear. For us, the reason is Jesus. It is because of the love that the Father has for the Son, and because we are found in the Son, that we have no reason to fear. There is no condemnation for us.

Because there is no condemnation now that we are in Jesus, the writer of Hebrews assures us that we can 'approach God's throne of grace with confidence, so that we may receive mercy and find grace to help us in our time of need'.[18]

If the one who could condemn us, who is justified in condemning us, does not, then what should we fear from others? Paul continues to the Romans: 'If God is for us, who can be against us?'[19]

It is our confidence in Jesus, in whom we can stand unafraid, which gives us the confidence not to fear others. Step two to being restored is to learn, even when we are afraid, that our advantage is that we stand with the God of angel armies. We can then allow him to calm our fears.

3. David restores Mephibosheth's land and gives him a seat at his table

The third thing that draws our attention in this scene is that David announces: 'I will surely show you kindness for the sake of your father Jonathan. I will restore to you all the land that belonged to your grandfather Saul, and you will always eat at my table.'[20]

Because of the love that David had for Jonathan, this was the least that he could do. Again, what must this have felt like for Mephibosheth? He has been acknowledged and reassured that he is not going to die. He has already been shown mercy. Here he is being given grace, the thing that he had no right to ask for and had not dared to expect. If, at the moment his life was spared, he could have walked out the door, he would have been a happy man; but he receives far more from David. He receives grace. Max Lucado writes: 'David could have sent money to Lo Debar. A lifelong annuity would have generously fulfilled his promise. But David gave Mephibosheth more than a pension, he gave him a place – a place at the royal table.'[21]

A seat at the table was more than Mephibosheth deserved. He was more than simply another dinner guest. David was bringing him into the family; he was bringing him into relationship. Mephibosheth was taking Jonathan's space in David's heart. He was family. We see that at the end of the chapter: 'So Mephibosheth ate at David's table like one of the king's sons.'[22]

Grace is undeserved in that we ourselves can do nothing to provoke it or to remove it, but that doesn't mean it is without reason. When we are brought into the heart of God as his children, we are taking the space of Jesus in the heart of God. We become family. We are not given a religious pension that we cash in at the appropriate time so we can get on with singing our hymns and going to church on Sundays. We are given a seat at the table, a space in the heart; we have joined the family. When I was baptized, the Bible verse that was given to me was 1 John 3:1: 'See what great love the Father has lavished on us, that we should be called children of God! And that is what we are!'[23]

We are not objects of pity, not slaves, not even honoured guests. We are God's children.

That's grace. I know that there is nothing I have done in my life that could earn me a seat at that table as an honoured guest, let alone as a son. There have been plenty of things that I feel would disqualify me from a seat. But no matter what I have done or failed to do, I have chosen to place my trust, my hope, my love and my life in Christ. He is my Lord, and has become my Brother, and so I find myself at his table. I am both bewildered and joyful to be here, as I am sure many of you are too. And yet he loves me, he welcomes me, he delights in me, he invites me. As Philip Yancey puts it in his timeless book *What's So Amazing about Grace?*: 'Grace declares that we are still God's pride and joy.'[24]

We live in a world where mercy is lacking, let alone grace. In this world, grace is scandalous. What's so amazing about grace, we ask with Philip Yancey? It's amazing because it takes a dead dog and seats him at the table of the king as a son. It takes people like you and me and allows us to be called *children of God*. And that is what we are! Grace seeks out the forgotten, is tender to the broken, is restorative to the dispossessed and is adoptive of the orphan. What's so amazing about grace? The fact that there is nothing you can do to make God love you more, and nothing you can do to make him love you less. You are invited regardless.

Step three to being restored is to take your place at the table as a child of the King.

There is so much more that I could say about this. So much more that we could dive into in the depths of Scripture. To end the chapter, though, I want us to reflect and be challenged. In many ways, I have tried to encourage us to look at this story from the position of Mephibosheth, but what about if we were to look at it from the position of David?

Is there someone today who you could show kindness to? And for whose sake would you show that kindness? For Jesus' sake. He said: 'Truly I tell you, whatever you did for one of the least of these brothers and sisters of mine, you did for me.'[25]

So we ask ourselves, as David did: is there anyone to whom I can show God's kindness? The kindness and grace we have freely received we are now called to freely give.

Who can I recognize and call by name today, showing them their value and worth when they feel devoid of value and worth?

Who can I reassure today, calming their fears when they fear the worst?

Who can I show grace to today, welcoming them to my table in order that they might feel truly part of the family?

As was the case with Mephibosheth, it might not be someone you expect. Jesus, when at a dinner party himself, said:

> When you give a luncheon or dinner, do not invite your friends, your brothers or sisters, your relatives, or your rich neighbours; if you do, they may invite you back and so you will be repaid. But when you give a banquet, invite the poor, the crippled, the lame, the blind, and you will be blessed. Although they cannot repay you, you will be repaid at the resurrection of the righteous.[26]

Do you show kindness and grace to those who deserve it, or those who feel they have earned it? Or do you show grace to those who are undeserving? Who might those people be in your community? Like David, don't wait for them to come to you. Look for them, seek them out and welcome them, just as you and I have been sought and welcomed.

Yes, Lord King, even a dead dog like me.

Questions for Reflection

1. Are there people in your life who 'see' you? How does that affect the way you respond to them?

2. Grace (*hesed*) is costly. Have you experienced the kind of sacrificial love that David shows Mephibosheth?

3. The place where Mephibosheth lived was called Lo Debar, meaning 'no pasture' or 'no word'. Either suggests a place of despair. What is *your* Lo Debar that leads you to feelings of isolation and worthlessness?

4. How can we show others wrestling with these feelings the same grace that David showed Mephibosheth?

5. How can we receive that grace ourselves?

7

Balcony Choices

In the spring, at the time when kings go off to war, David sent Joab out with the king's men and the whole Israelite army. They destroyed the Ammonites and besieged Rabbah. But David remained in Jerusalem.

One evening David got up from his bed and walked around on the roof of the palace. From the roof he saw a woman washing. The woman was very beautiful, and David sent someone to find out about her. The man said, 'She is Bathsheba, the daughter of Eliam and the wife of Uriah the Hittite.' Then David sent messengers to get her. She came to him, and he slept with her. (Now she was purifying herself from her monthly uncleanness.) Then she went back home. The woman conceived and sent word to David, saying, 'I am pregnant.'[1]

As we come to this part of the story, the tone seems to change. Many other writers and scholars acknowledge that this is the turning point in the story of David. So much of what we have seen in previous chapters has been positive for David: it is clear that even when David was not able to defeat his enemies in his own strength, or when the odds seemed stacked against him, God stepped in and together they overcame the challenges. David the shepherd boy, the youngest of the family, is now firmly established as the king of a united nation. But here we come face to face with David's weakness – with our human weakness.

If we are seeking to learn lessons from David's life, then those lessons are to be found not just in his victories or successes but also in his areas of weakness and failings, because we too know what it is like to be in these places. If we are honest, there are times when we can identify much more with this part of David's story than we can with other parts.

David Was in the Wrong Place at the Wrong Time

Have you ever been in the wrong place at the wrong time?

The most fateful example I have heard of this is the story of the Japanese businessman Tsutomu Yamaguchi.

At 8:15 a.m. on 6 August 1945, Tsutomu Yamaguchi was 200 miles away from home on a business trip to Hiroshima. He worked for Mitsubishi Heavy Industries and had only arrived in the city that day. As he was getting out of a taxi, he saw a plane pass overhead, and as he stared up at the sky he noticed two parachutes. A moment later the first atomic bomb, called 'Little Boy', exploded around 2 miles from where Tsutomu stood. Despite the 2-mile distance, the intense flash of heat burned him badly across his stomach, and the blast from the explosion ruptured his eardrums as well as temporarily blinding him.

He managed to make his way down to a bomb shelter, where he was cared for by other survivors. Tsutomu was simply in the wrong place at the wrong time, and was well enough to return home the next day to his home town of Nagasaki.

On 9 August, just three days later, Tsutomu was able to make it in to work. At the exact moment that he was explaining to his boss how Little Boy had destroyed Hiroshima, he saw the same white flash out of the office window. 'Fat Man', the second atomic bomb, had just detonated over the city.

Tsutomu Yamaguchi is the only officially recognized survivor of the two atomic bomb explosions, and probably qualifies as the most direct example of being in the wrong place at the wrong time.

Let's look at 2 Samuel 11:1 for a moment: 'In the spring, at the time when kings go off to war, David sent Joab out with the king's men and the whole Israelite army. They destroyed the Ammonites and besieged Rabbah. But David remained in Jerusalem.'

Right here at the start of our passage we see that David is also in the wrong place at the wrong time. Not by accident or unhappy coincidence like Tsutomu Yamaguchi, but because that's where he chooses to be.

This was not the time for David to be sitting around[2] at home; this was a time when kings would lead their troops into battle. The spring marked the end of the cold and wet winter weather and the first possibility for military campaigns, which were usually led by warrior leaders such as David. This was what kings did.

So, it is the time of year when all the kings go off to war, but this king, King David, remains in Jerusalem with a dangerous amount of free time on his hands. David is no longer being what kings broadly were in those days – a projection of strength and power to show his own people, and the world around, that Israel remained a dominant force in the area. But David is also failing to be the kind of king that Israel had asked for in the first place. If we go back to 1 Samuel 8:20, to the time before Saul is anointed as king, we read the job description for what the people wanted: 'We want a king over us. Then we shall be like all the other nations, with a king to lead us and to go out before us and fight our battles.'[3]

When we think about the rest of the story, how it escalates and takes on a momentum all of its own, we can see that David first gets into danger because he is not where he is meant to be. David is in the wrong place at the wrong time.

I wonder, as we reflect on the story of David in this passage, how often it is the same for us? It does seem to be that whenever we are in the wrong place, things start to unravel!

Whether we find ourselves with the wrong crowd of friends, getting involved in something that we know we shouldn't; whether it is sitting in front of the TV or computer when we should be asleep or with our family; whether it is engaging with gossips at work – how often is it that being in the wrong place at the wrong time leads us down a road where life takes on a momentum of its own?

It doesn't have to be an actual place either, because I get the impression in this story that David is not in the right place with *God*. The hunger to do what is right before God above all else; the hunger to pursue God, to be open to the leading of God; the hunger to follow God wherever he leads – I don't see it in David here.

Perhaps David had climbed too high? Max Lucado points this out in his chapter on this passage: 'It's possible to ascend too far, stand too tall, and elevate too much.'[4] Max reminds us that when we spend too long being too high, it affects our senses.

I remember going through a phase of being fascinated by expeditions to climb Mount Everest, the world's tallest mountain. What is it that makes Everest such a challenging mountain to climb? It is not the most difficult technically; much smaller mountains provide a far greater technical challenge for a climber. What makes Everest such a challenge is, of course, its height. With a summit at 8,848.86 metres above sea level, Everest requires climbers to reach the cruising altitude of a commercial airliner, and in doing so they enter something known in climbing circles as the 'death zone'. The death zone is generally recognized as an altitude above 8,000 metres, where the human body, even with supplementary oxygen, will start to die. At that height, our brains don't get enough oxygen, and so our decision-making is impaired; the extreme effort that it takes to walk, requiring around eight breaths per step, together with the extreme cold, means that climbers are in danger of slips or falls in this perilous environment. To put it bluntly, we were not made to survive in this environment; we were not made to be this high for this long.

Perhaps the same is true for David? He has reached a point in his reign where he is at the height of his power. However, even this great king cannot live this high for this long without having his judgement impaired and risking slips or falls. His story is a warning to those who are in positions of power and authority, whether at national or local level. We need to make sure we come down the mountain in order to survive.

David's power leads him to neglect his relationship with God, to stop paying attention to the attitude of his heart before God. Things can unravel for us, too, when we are in the wrong place with God.

Wherever we have chosen to neglect our relationship with God, not running after him with all that we are, not relying on his strength and his leading for us; whenever we start to put our own opinions and choices, our own power and abilities, over and above the best that God has for us, we too are in danger of slips and falls. Our judgement also suffers.

David finds himself standing on a balcony looking at Bathsheba instead of being with his troops in battle. The balcony takes the place of the battlefield (although in this story, as we will see in a moment, the balcony becomes the battlefield). So, for a moment, let's put ourselves in David's shoes and ask: where are *our* 'balconies'? Where are those dangerous places for us? Where are the wrong place/wrong time moments in our lives?

For David, his balcony was a literal one, in Jerusalem. What about us? Where are the places we find ourselves in, perhaps on a day-to-day basis, where we know, hand on heart, we shouldn't be?

David Wanted What He Couldn't Have

The year after my first book, *When Rain Falls Like Lead*, was published in 2013, I did something of a lecture tour around different churches in the south of England to speak on the question 'Where is God when we suffer?' I remember speaking at a church where a friend of ours is the minister, and the plan was to have a morning service, starting informally with a bit of breakfast, including pastries and croissants. I love croissants, so if I ever happen to be at your church then I won't say no to that format. On this particular occasion, we had already eaten breakfast as guests in someone's home, so I didn't want to offend our friends who had hosted us by scoffing down a load of croissants. For this reason, I decided to try and avoid the tasty refreshments provided by the church. I was talking to some people before the service as everyone was gathering, and just as the food was brought out to the tables one of the deacons came up to let me know that it was time to meet to pray before the service started. What threw me was that he used the good charismatic phrase: 'Let's get you filled!' I said to Bex on the drive home, 'Is it bad that I hoped he was offering me a croissant?!'

There is something about us that wants what we can't have. Just ask Adam and Eve.

David wanted what he couldn't have, and one of the roots of wanting what we cannot have is entitlement. It is thinking that we deserve it, that somehow we are owed it. For whatever reason, we think we have 'arrived', and because we have arrived there are certain things that should come with that. If you get a promotion at work you expect a bigger salary, or a bigger office, or more prestige. After all, you've earned it. Right?

God had raised David from the status of a shepherd to the status of a king, which is one heck of a promotion. David might have been forgiven for thinking that, now that he had 'arrived' at the destination God had planned for him, there would be certain perks of the job – things he was entitled to, things he deserved.

Perhaps the same could be said for the UK politicians who fell foul of the British public due to an expenses scandal in which certain Members of Parliament were claiming money from the taxpayer for things they should not have been claiming for. A famous example was one MP who claimed tax-payers' money to create an artificial island to house the ducks in his pond.

Or consider the American politicians who claimed it was essential to use private jets to fly around the country for visits and meetings, all at the expense of the US taxpayer.

Ask any of these people why they did it, and perhaps the answer you would get, if they were brave enough to say it out loud, is that they felt it was what they were entitled to.

What about us? What do we feel we are entitled to? Entitlement comes when we first feel that something is lacking and then believe there is something that can fill the void. For example, we may feel that we are entitled to be happy, but at this moment we are not happy. We then spend our time going after whatever will fill that void and make us happy.

In his book on David, R.T. Kendall highlights a particular working out of this view in this account of David's life, which is relevant to some today. He writes: 'Sex is a physical need. It is so easy to rationalise about our physical needs. Eve saw that the fruit was good to eat, and since God had made her with an appetite, it would not be wrong to eat the fruit. In the same way people today rationalise adultery.'[5]

For David, the temptation he fell to was sex. But replace the word 'sex' with anything else that you feel tempted by, and very often the rationale stands up in our minds: *there is something I'm entitled to; I'm not getting it; so I will go out and get it.*

So many relationships have been sacrificed on the altar of this seemingly rational and yet tragically entitled mindset.

For David, as king, this woman bathing was what he felt entitled to. After all, he was the king. This has been the mark of so many men in power. Famously, in the 2016 US presidential race, audiotapes emerged of then Republican candidate Donald Trump bragging to a TV host that because of who he was, he could get women to do whatever he wanted, and that he could do whatever he wanted with women. He felt entitled, and that entitlement led him to take what he wanted. Surprisingly, this man went on to become the 45th President of the United States.

Another problem for David, as we look at him wanting what he couldn't have, was that he abdicated responsibility, which we see in 2 Samuel 11:2.

David sent Joab to do the job for him. He offloaded the responsibility to Joab when the responsibility was his. He has gone from being the hands-on king of the people, the servant of God with a heart after God's own heart, to being an aloof king who sends people to do his bidding. He goes from serving God to playing God.

I wonder if you have noticed a funny thing about the phrase 'playing God'. Whenever we use that phrase, the God we are talking about, the God we are playing, looks nothing like the God we see revealed in the gospels.

So when we are thinking about wanting what we cannot have (or 'coveting', to use an older word for it), the God we are playing is very different from the God whom we see revealed in Jesus. Philippians 2:6–8 says that Jesus:

> being in very nature God,
>> did not consider equality with God something to be used
>> to his own advantage;
> rather, he made himself nothing
>> by taking the very nature of a servant,
>> being made in human likeness.

And being found in appearance as a man,
>   he humbled himself
>   by becoming obedient to death –
>   even death on a cross![6]

The King of Kings, the one who is exalted to the highest place, the one before whom every knee will bow, didn't push to have everything he thought was owed to him. Instead, he took the place of a servant and put others first. He embraced all of who he was in God.

That was one of the ways David went wrong in our Scripture passage. He thought he was owed something, and he grasped hold of it, even though it wasn't his. He put himself first. He gave away his responsibility to be a man after God's heart, to be the servant king, the king who weeps with his people, the king who celebrates with his people, the king who stands with his people in battle; and he became a king who dominated and abused his people – starting with Bathsheba. Notice that in the twenty-seven verses of this passage, Bathsheba is referred to by name on only one occasion, in verse 3: 'David sent someone to find out about her. The man said, "She is Bathsheba, the daughter of Eliam and the wife of Uriah the Hittite."'[7]

Bathsheba is depersonalized to some extent here. To David she is simply a naked woman bathing on the roof who he wants to have sex with. Three times in this account she is simply described as 'the/a woman', three times more than she is referred to by name.

I wonder if we can put ourselves in David's shoes for a moment and ask: have we ever wanted something that was not ours to have? Another person's car, or spouse, or life? Have we ever thought we were entitled to something that we knew, hand on heart, was not ours to have?

Have we ever offloaded the responsibility for doing the right thing to other people? Have we been tempted to think: I don't need to invest in my marriage, or the upbringing of my kids. I don't need to invest in making sure my workplace is a good and healthy place to work in. I don't need to be the one who contributes to the body of Christ, reflecting the love and unity that we see modelled in God as Father, Son and Holy Spirit. There are others who can do that.

One of the problems we have in our society today is not so much having things; it is having to have things. It is a way of thinking. We say to ourselves: *my life will be complete if I have such-and-such*, and then we pursue that thing with all our energy and time and resources. We even convince ourselves that the things we want are a matter of life and death – because if something is a matter of life and death, then it's pretty easy to justify. Or to put it another way, when it feels like a matter of life and death, you can justify doing, or taking, just about anything.

Sin is essentially un-relational. It is the thing that breaks my relationships: with God, with others and with myself. I might be able to justify it in my mind, but there is always a cost to sin, and that cost is always relational. Why is that important? Up to this point we have used the language of 'can't have', but what about those who *can* take what they want? If it's simply about 'can't have', then when you have the power to take what you want, the sky's the limit, right? In some ways it might seem easier when it is something you can't have. I might want a yacht, but I'm very unlikely to get one, and I'm even less likely to take one. The issue here is that by focusing on what I can't have, I am doing two significant things.

First, I am devaluing what I already have by giving myself the impression that it is not enough.

Second, I am developing a mindset that makes taking this next step much more likely: taking what I *can* take. The frustration of wanting what you can't have builds to the point where you get the fulfilment by taking what you *can*. That becomes about power, and it is the same issue that Donald Trump struggled with, which he revealed to us in that recording, and it was the same issue that David struggled with.

What it then comes down to is not 'can I', but '*should* I'? Is this good for me? Is this the best that God has for me? If sin is un-relational, then it is because God is relational; God represents perfect relationship as Father, Son and Holy Spirit. So, does this thing that I am wanting enhance and protect my relationships – with God, with others and with myself – or does it harm or break them?

Perhaps you have already taken several steps down a road that you know, hand on heart, isn't the best that God has for you. Perhaps you are already seeing your relationships suffer. But it is not too late to turn around and walk away. It is not too late to prioritize relationship over the things you feel you must have. It is not too late to step off the balcony and stop looking at Bathsheba.

David Tried to Cover Up His Mistakes

David had made a series of mistakes that led him to this moment in the story. He was in the wrong place at the wrong time, and he wanted what he couldn't have. He should have turned back at several points in the story, but he kept going, and the story takes on a life of its own. Bathsheba becomes pregnant, and all of a sudden David's mistakes have caught up with him. Once again, he has a choice. Does he own those mistakes, or does he try to cover them up? David goes for the cover-up and tries to make it look as if Bathsheba is pregnant by her own husband, Uriah. When that doesn't work, he tries to get rid of the problem by having Uriah killed in battle:

> In the morning David wrote a letter to Joab and sent it with Uriah. In it he wrote, 'Put Uriah out in front where the fighting is fiercest. Then withdraw from him so that he will be struck down and die.'
>
> So while Joab had the city under siege, he put Uriah at a place where he knew the strongest defenders were. When the men of the city came out and fought against Joab, some of the men in David's army fell; moreover, Uriah the Hittite died.[8]

For a man who penned some of the most beautiful words in the Bible, which many of us read on a daily basis, this is a terrible comedown; here, David is writing his story in Uriah's blood. There is a famous saying: 'The pen is mightier than the sword,' and here that is exactly what David is doing: using his pen as a sword.

It is no surprise that there are two names we always link with David: Goliath and Bathsheba. In the story of Bathsheba, David came face to face with a giant far more fearsome than Goliath, but this time, it was the giant who came out on top. This time it was the giant that defeated David.

I wonder if we can put ourselves in David's shoes again and ask: what do we do when we come face to face with our weaknesses? The world may tell you that there are two types of people when it comes to weaknesses: those who have them, and those who don't. This was a line I was told by my grandfather when I was growing up, and one that has taken decades to unravel, because that type of thinking hasn't taken me anywhere good. However, in my experience there *are* two types of people when it comes to weaknesses: those who are self-aware enough to know they have them, and those who aren't. Because we all have weaknesses.

We have all had times in our lives when we have made wrong choices, whether those choices have a big impact or a smaller impact. We all make mistakes. That is part of our humanity, and God knows it; there is no hiding it from him. Sometimes we find ourselves in situations that we never planned to be in; or with consequences we never expected to be faced with.

What do we do when those moments come? What do we do when we come face to face with our weaknesses? The temptation is to cover up our weaknesses and our mistakes – to think we can deal with them on our own. I know that from my own life. Perhaps it was due to the impact of those words spoken to me as a child, which made me feel we should never show weakness. There have been times in my life when I have tried to cover up my mistakes, when I have tried to fix and deal with my weaknesses on my own. It never worked out well.

When we cover up our mistakes, when we fail to deal with them, they only get worse; they only bring us more trouble and more pain. They take on a life of their own, a dark energy which gains momentum the longer we leave those things un-dealt with: a powerful shadow side.

The thing to understand about those hidden and un-dealt-with mistakes is that they will always find a way to come out. In some respects, that's God's grace towards us, because those hidden mistakes which we try to deal with on our own become a disease of the soul. It's a disease that eats us up inside, and destroys us with worry, guilt, shame and fear, a little piece at a time, a day at a time. A slow fade into a living death.

That is not what God wants for us. God wants us to live, to know the fullness and vibrancy and freedom that his life for us can bring. Jesus himself said: 'I have come that they may have life, and have it to the full.'[9] He offers us that life each and every day, but we have to choose it. Choosing it is not a line that we cross once, after which everything is magically easy, with no problems or weaknesses.

In Deuteronomy 30, Moses gathers the people together and speaks God's words to them, words that are spoken to us today:

> This day I call the heavens and the earth as witnesses against you that I have set before you life and death, blessings and curses. Now choose life, so that you and your children may live and that you may love the LORD your God, listen to his voice, and hold fast to him. For the LORD is your life, and he will give you many years in the land he swore to give to your fathers, Abraham, Isaac and Jacob.[10]

Every day, we are confronted with life and death, blessings and curses, and we are invited to choose life. We are invited to choose blessing. When it comes to the mistakes we have made, part of taking hold of that life is owning up to our mistakes, admitting to them, so that God can make us right with him and with those around us.

So, in our weaknesses, let us hold on to God, hold fast to him; for it is he, and not the things we chase, who is our life.

God Is a God of Grace

Many people think that David wrote a psalm about this time in his life:

> Have mercy on me, O God,
>> according to your unfailing love;
> according to your great compassion
>> blot out my transgressions.
> Wash away all my iniquity
>> and cleanse me from my sin.
> For I know my transgressions,
>> and my sin is always before me.
> Against you, you only, have I sinned
>> and done what is evil in your sight;
> so you are right in your verdict
>> and justified when you judge.
> Surely I was sinful at birth,
>> sinful from the time my mother conceived me.
> Yet you desired faithfulness even in the womb;
>> you taught me wisdom in that secret place.
> Cleanse me with hyssop, and I shall be clean;
>> wash me, and I shall be whiter than snow.
> Let me hear joy and gladness;
>> let the bones you have crushed rejoice.
> Hide your face from my sins
>> and blot out all my iniquity.
> Create in me a pure heart, O God,
>> and renew a steadfast spirit within me.[11]

God's grace was shown in this story. We see it when God showed David his mistakes by sending the prophet Nathan to him (see 2 Sam. 12). But we also see it in the way God hears David's prayer. The next sentence in the prayer reads:

> Do not cast me from your presence
> or take your Holy Spirit from me.[12]

David is not cast off, and the Spirit of God's anointing stays on David.

In Acts 13:22 we read how God sees David: 'After removing Saul, he made David their king. God testified concerning him: "I have found David son of Jesse, a man after my own heart; he will do everything I want him to do."'

God describes David as a man after his own heart. This always gives me a great amount of encouragement, because David messes up. When I think of the great women and men in the Bible, they too know what it is to make mistakes: Moses, Sarah, Mary Magdalene, Peter . . . to name a few. And yet they are still part of the story. In fact, when we read through the genealogy at the start of Matthew's gospel, Bathsheba is one of four women who are mentioned alongside Mary the mother of Jesus: Tamar, Rahab, Ruth and 'the wife of Uriah'. These are women with questionable pasts, but they are in the story. God's grace is not so small that it is diminished by our mistakes, in the same way that the love of parents for their children is not diminished by their kids' mistakes. The high-water mark of the love of God, the highest it reaches, is the point where he lavishes it on us as his children.

Here in 2 Samuel 11, David's choices on the balcony took him away from the best that God had for him, but they did not take him away from God's heart, from God's mercy or from God's grace.

In 2 Timothy 2:13 we read this: 'If we are faithless, he remains faithful, for he cannot disown himself.'[13]

God is the God of mercy, the God of grace, the God of love, the God who forgives, the God who brings us into his heart for all eternity. This is who he is! So even in the face of our mistakes, he cannot *not* be who he is!

Our choices, the choices we make on the balconies of our lives, can sometimes take us away from the best that God has for us, but they never take us away from the heart of God; or from the mercy of God; or from the grace of God.

When we come to God and admit our mistakes, he can cleanse us from them, and as David prayed, make us as white as snow.

When we stop focusing on what we have to have, even the things we can't have, he can put a right spirit in us.

When we ask him to guide us towards life and the best that he has for us, so that we don't find ourselves in the wrong place at the wrong time, then he can create in us a clean heart, a heart to be where he is, a heart to be like him, a heart to choose his life, each and every day.

Then we, like David, will be a people after his own heart too.

Questions for Reflection

1. Are you good at learning from your mistakes? Or from other people's?

2. Where do you turn when a situation seems to be unravelling?

3. Things start to go wrong for David because he is not where he is meant to be. Are you somewhere God doesn't want you to be? Are you listening to him to guide you?

4. Do you have a safety net if you find yourself in a wrong time/wrong place situation?

5. Do you recognize a sense of entitlement in your life?

6. I say in this chapter that covering up our mistakes ultimately leads to 'a disease of the soul'. What might that look like?

7. Is there a person or group to whom you can be accountable and share safely some personal struggles?

8. Our choices sometimes take us away from the best God has for us, but they never take us away from the heart of God. Read Psalm 51 and ask God where he needs to bring you in line with his heart.

8

'I Will Not Give to the Lord That Which Has Cost Me Nothing'

With all that has been said about David by writers and commentators on Scripture, it is perhaps what he wrote himself that we engage with most readily. This may be because, in his precious and intimate songs, we see something of the heart of the king. Not his battles, his conquests, his palaces, or even the drama of his mistakes, but his heart. Isn't that the journey we have been on? We wish not only to learn lessons from David's life but also to catch a glimpse of his heart. There is an honesty to the Psalms that you wouldn't see in the writings of any other head of state. There is a vulnerability to them which has the ability to break down our barriers and allow us somehow to own these words for ourselves.

There is so much that has been said about the Psalms, and even more that could be said, but in the interest of discipleship, and of exploring them as a way of learning lessons for our lives, I want to focus on them not simply as ancient liturgy or praise, but as a costly self-giving that is lived out in the ordinary reality of our lives.

But before we get to the Psalms, there are a couple of stories about David that give us an insight into his heart of worship.

On that day Gad went to David and said to him, 'Go up and build an altar to the LORD on the threshing floor of Araunah the Jebusite.' So David went up, as the LORD had commanded through Gad. When Araunah looked and saw the king and his officials coming towards him, he went out and bowed down before the king with his face to the ground.

Araunah said, 'Why has my lord the king come to his servant?'

'To buy your threshing floor,' David answered, 'so that I can build an altar to the LORD, that the plague on the people may be stopped.'

Araunah said to David, 'Let my lord the king take whatever he wishes and offer it up. Here are oxen for the burnt offering, and here are threshing-sledges and ox yokes for the wood. Your Majesty, Araunah gives all this to the king.' Araunah also said to him, 'May the LORD your God accept you.'

But the king replied to Araunah, 'No, I insist on paying you for it. I will not sacrifice to the LORD my God burnt offerings that cost me nothing.'

So David bought the threshing-floor and the oxen and paid fifty shekels of silver for them. David built an altar to the LORD there and sacrificed burnt offerings and fellowship offerings. Then the LORD answered his prayer on behalf of the land, and the plague on Israel was stopped.[1]

I don't know how well you know this story, but over the years it has become a significant one for me. I have been blessed to experience seasons of worship within my life of both joy and lament, of thankfulness and brokenness; but the one thing I believe strongly about worship in each of these seasons is that there is, and must be, a cost to it. We cannot simply go through the motions. We dare not give to the Lord that which has cost us nothing.

Worship Is God-Centred

It might sound like a simple thing to say, but worship is vital. Worship is God-centred. It is not primarily about *me*. Only God is worthy of praise, and as those who follow Jesus, who are his disciples, we need to make sure that he is at the centre of our worship.

I say this because I know how easy it is for other things to take God's place. Some will come to church and sing the hymns because what they really worship is tradition. Some will come to church and sing the songs because what they really worship is the band. Some will come to church and get lost in it all because what they really worship is the emotional response that all of it triggers.

I am sure there are other situations you can think of, but hopefully you see my point. We can come to church and we can sing *about* God; we might even sing *to* God; but is God at the centre? Is he the goal? Is he the focus of our worship?

The Westminster Catechism says: 'Man's chief end is to glorify God and enjoy him forever.' In other words, the first priority, the greatest goal, the very reason why we are here is to glorify God, to magnify God, to worship God. But the catechism also hints at something deeper within worship: relationship. Surely that is what the word 'enjoy' hints at? There can be no relationship without the giving of yourself, without it costing you something.

In another story, this time from 2 Samuel 6, we learn of David bringing the ark of the covenant back to Jerusalem and worshipping in celebration in front of the people. The writer tells us that David 'danced before the LORD with all his might'.[2] Later, we read that David's wife wasn't pleased with his dancing (something that I'm sure a lot of wives could relate to); but her issue was that it was undignified for a king to be 'leaping and dancing before the LORD'.[3] You can read the story yourself, but for me as I read it, what stands out clearly is that at the centre of David's praise, the centre of David's joy and the centre of David's worship was the Lord. Worship for David, and for us, must not be part of a religious checklist; it must be the giving of who we are, in every circumstance, to God in relationship.

The context of this passage is also helpful to us as we seek to understand the significance of what David was doing, and it highlights how important it was to have God at the centre of his worship.

David is bringing the ark of the Lord up to Jerusalem, to the capital. The ark of the Lord, the ark of the covenant, contained Aaron's staff that budded, the golden pot containing manna, and the stone tablets of the Ten Commandments. It was the presence of God among the people. The ark had moved from place to place, but David wanted it to have a permanent home – a home for the Lord among his people. David wanted to be near the presence of God, and he wanted the people to be near the presence of God. In fact, his desire to have God at the centre of their life was so strong that he could not rest until he had found a place for him.

What is God-centred worship about? We can sometimes be very quick to reel off passages such as Romans 12:1, which says: 'Therefore, I urge you, brothers and sisters, in view of God's mercy, to offer your bodies as a living sacrifice, holy and pleasing to God – this is your true and proper worship,' and then state that everything we are is an act of worship. That is true. It is something that the Psalms attest to, and something that the church throughout the ages has highlighted. So, if this is what you believe, then I want to assure you that you have a healthy view of what worship is. However, I would also like to ask you: what does that actually mean? What does a God-centred life of worship look like? This is the challenge that each of us needs to explore seven days a week. It's easier on a Sunday in church because it can feel as though we have already been led part of the way into the throne room. But what does it look like when you are on the school run, when you are at work, when you are at home, when you're up late at night?

I don't have space to explore all of those scenarios with you here. But what I do want to do is to encourage you to explore this for yourself. What we can see as a heart characteristic, and as a life lesson for us, is that David longed for the presence of God, longing so hard that he could not rest until he had entered that presence.

He wanted to place God at the centre, because he knew that he could neither glorify God nor enjoy him unless God took his rightful place at the centre of government, the centre of national focus, the centre of religious activity and the centre of his life.

I wonder: how often do we long for God like that? How often do we really want to put God at the centre? How often do we say, 'Lord, I cannot lie down or find any peace until I have made a place for you at the centre of my life'?

Worship leader and songwriter Matt Redman, writing in *Premier Christianity* magazine in February 2021, says:

> When we say: 'Let it be "on earth as it is in heaven"' . . . we are asking that Christ would be at the centre, and everything else – our lives, homes, towns and even nations – would be arranged around him and his majesty. True worship, then, is a life that prioritizes the worth of God above all else, and then demonstrates that worth through all of our thoughts, words and actions.[4]

The extravagant procession that brings the ark into the city in 2 Samuel 6 is amazing, and must have been incredible to see, but it was an extension of having God at the centre; and the reason for all those celebrations was because God *was* finally at the centre. It is the same for us, too, as we seek to live our lives in the likeness of Christ and as we seek to learn lessons from David's life. We do so, knowing that the amazing transformations we long to see, the lives we want to have, come as an extension of having God at the centre.

Worship Is Extravagant

Let's stick with the story in 2 Samuel 6 for a moment longer. What we see as we look at David's response is that worship is extravagant.

We can see this extravagance shine through even more clearly when we look at the context of this passage. David wasn't just another guy in the crowd able to slip into anonymity. He was the king; he had a public image to protect. He was a man who had been given more power, wealth and responsibility than we could ever imagine. And yet, despite the power, the wealth, the standing and the image, David led the way, losing himself so publicly in his worship, being so on fire for God, that it burned away his inhibitions and pride.

But sometimes extravagance doesn't come with what you give, but in what you give up for God. In David, we can see both.

In terms of what David gave, we see the extravagance of sacrifice: 'When those who were carrying the ark of the LORD had taken six steps, he sacrificed a bull and a fattened calf.'[5]

We also see the extravagance of the gifts that he gave to the people: 'Then he gave a loaf of bread, a cake of dates and a cake of raisins to each person in the whole crowd of Israelites, both men and women.'[6]

Part of this extravagance was also in what he gave up. He gave up his inhibitions, his pride and his self-opinion.

Have you ever been in a service where you have looked around and seen how others are worshipping freely, or been in a prayer gathering where others are praying freely, losing themselves in love of their Saviour? Perhaps you thought, *I wish I could do that*, but you haven't. There is something that stops us, isn't there? Something that holds us back. Part of the extravagance in worship that we see here with David is the heart that gives up on those attitudes and steps out in reckless abandon. Oswald Chambers said: 'The consequence of abandonment never enters into our outlook because our lives are so taken up in Him.'[7]

There are times when this really challenges us, because so often the consequences of abandonment are the things that stay in our minds.

How are we going to look?

What will people think?

And yet we have a God who is gracious enough that he still calls us deeper. He calls us into a more intimate relationship, a more holistic expression of worship, where extravagance finds its place.

Worship is about everything that we are, magnifying everything that God is. It is the intimate enjoyment of a child enjoying their heavenly Parent. As Pete Greig writes: 'The deeper we receive our identity as "dearly loved children", the greater our desire to spend time with our Father in prayer.'[8]

If we wonder where this extravagant worship comes from, it is born from God's extravagance towards us. In other words, if we have a God who has not even spared his only Son, but given him as an extravagant sacrifice, then should we not, in response to that, give our worship extravagantly to him?

I think this is what David is doing here: he is giving extravagant worship. He was totally consumed with God and didn't care what others thought.

Jesus says: 'A good man brings good things out of the good stored up in his heart, and an evil man brings evil things out of the evil stored up in his heart. For the mouth speaks what the heart is full of.'[9] And in the same way, out of what is stored up in our hearts, we sing, we serve and we live. That is what David's dancing is about here. It's not about showing off, or getting so caught up in the hype that you don't know what you're doing. It was an overflow of abundance of love that he had for God in his heart. And this is the lesson for us as well. The worship that we give, in the midst of hype and what others are doing, needs to be an overflow of the extravagance of love that we have in our hearts for Jesus. It's not a show for the eyes of others. It's about relationship expressing itself in the highest way.

Worship Is Often Opposed

It's worth mentioning again the reaction of David's wife Michal to David's worship. Scripture tells us that when she saw what David did 'she despised him in her heart'.[10]

When David gets home, he gets an earful from his queen: 'When David returned home to bless his household, Michal daughter of Saul came out to meet him and said, "How the king of Israel has distinguished himself today, going around half-naked in full view of the slave girls of his servants as any vulgar fellow would!"'[11]

Michal, being Saul's daughter, was raised in a palace, in the king's home. She has a very clear idea of what constitutes proper decorum and etiquette and behaviour. She knows how royals are supposed to act. All her life, she has been forced to maintain royal dignity and honour, sometimes during the most difficult of circumstances.

What David does offends her royal dignity and pride. Exhibitionists and show-offs may leap and dance, dressed in an ephod, but kings do not! Lower-class people, the 'vulgar' as she calls them, may shout and blow trumpets, but royals do not! Those who wear purple robes and golden crowns should always act with dignity and carry themselves with regal bearing. They should always act with restraint. They do not let themselves get carried away before the masses.

Michal could not understand that what David was doing, he did before the Lord. There may have been thousands there that day, but David was worshipping with an audience of one: the One.

Michal's response reminds us that the world continually opposes and fails to understand those who worship with extravagant abandon before the Lord.

The world dismisses those with commitment and dedication as being fools.

If our worship is about every area of our life being God-centred and extravagant, then we will face opposition. The media will often brand us as fanatics, our friends may think we have been brainwashed, and many others will question from a distance why it is that we do the things we do.

What happened to David eventually happens to everyone who does what he did before the Lord: the world opposes them or mocks them. Like Michal, the world does this because it does not understand. There are cultural and environmental barriers that hold back its ability to grasp what true worship really means, and what it means for those who seek to worship in that way.

Worship is not formulaic. It's much more about our hearts than about what we do. And often it is about losing in order to gain, laying down something in order to take up something else. What I mean is this: there are many times when we lose the things that define who we are, in order to be free in worship, but then God redefines us to show us who we truly are.

Do we let go of the culture that defines us, so that we can be free in worship and so that God may, through that worship, redefine who we really are as his children? Do we let go of the opinions of our families so that we can be free in worship and so that God may, through that worship, show us a better perspective on family?

Many of us have been brought up to think that certain things are acceptable, especially publicly, and certain things are not. So often, it is our culture, and not the Holy Spirit, that tells us what is and is not acceptable.

Is it OK to show high levels of emotion in public?

Is it OK to raise your hands in worship?

Is it OK to speak in tongues, prophesy and move in the gifts of the Spirit?

I think so.

Is it OK to dance semi-naked in worship to God in front of an entire city?

I think so too. But we answer that question a little more slowly and with a bit more hesitation, because it doesn't fit in with what culturally we find acceptable. We need to allow worship to impact our cultural views, so that it goes beyond skin-deep and into every part of who we are.

We used to live only a few miles from Brighton, in south-east England. One of the things I always loved to eat at the seaside was a type of candy called Brighton rock. It had to be mint-flavoured; all other flavours are an abomination! The interesting thing about a stick of rock is that it has a name, usually of the town where you bought it, running all the way down the middle. So, no matter where you break it open, you will see that word.

Imagine that your heart of worship is that word, and that your life is the stick of rock. If people were to break your life open, would they see your heart of worship? Would they see it if they broke open your work life? Or your family life? Or even your church life?

We are dealing with big things here, so it is vitally important that we allow the Holy Spirit to influence how we worship God. I believe it's only then that we will see it impact every area of our lives.

Should opposition deter us? Should it hinder our worship? I hope not. It *should not*. For I hope that, like David, we do it anyway. As David knew, and shows us here, what God thinks is far more important than what people think. If we focus on the negativity around us, and the opinions of those around us over God's, then the opposition to our worship will stifle our extravagance, and our desire to have God at the centre will decay.

But if we focus on what the Lord wants, then, as was the case with David, that opposition, although it may be ongoing, will not overcome us.

Psalms

Having laid a foundation of God-centred, extravagant worship that stands even in the face of opposition within the life of David, I want to spend a moment focusing on a couple of psalms – because it is one thing to have a theology or understanding of worship, but another thing to live that out in the reality of day-to-day life. I have really come to treasure in recent years the belief that all of Scripture can be lived out by ordinary people in ordinary times.

Thanksgiving

Shout for joy to the LORD, all the earth.
　　Worship the LORD with gladness;
　　come before him with joyful songs.

Know that the LORD is God.

It is he who made us, and we are his;

we are his people, the sheep of his pasture.

Enter his gates with thanksgiving

and his courts with praise;

give thanks to him and praise his name.

For the LORD is good and his love endures for ever;

his faithfulness continues through all generations.[12]

In his fantastic book *Praying the Psalms*, my friend Ian takes us through the Psalms and shows how we might use them as a rhythm of prayer for our lives. Reflecting on how static our worship can be, compared to the noisiness of the psalms of praise, he encourages us to hear the summons of the King: 'Through seven imperatives – make a joyful noise, worship, come, know, enter, give thanks, and bless – we are called to pilgrimage.'[13]

How do we approach thanksgiving? There are certainly many things, more than we could count, that we have as reasons to praise God. In fact, as the eighteenth-century hymn-writer Charles Wesley pleads:

O for a thousand tongues to sing

my great Redeemer's praise . . .

Even if I had a thousand tongues (and that's quite a picture), it would not be enough to sing the praises of such a wonderful and amazing God. In fact, according to Psalm 100, it takes 'all the earth' and 'all generations' to do justice to the Lord.

When we pray together as a family in the evening, before our son Leo goes to bed, we begin by saying 'thank you' to God. It's important to actively bring to mind the things that we are thankful for, because so often it creates a sense of perspective in our lives and reminds us that we have so much to be grateful for. The practice of doing this each day in prayer roots our thankfulness in the constancy of God, and not the ever-changing situations of our lives. There will be days when it is harder to bring things to mind, when times are tough and we struggle (we will come on to that shortly), but finding a moment to be thankful, even in those times, will begin to change the way we see the world around us.

David knew that he had so much to be thankful for. God had raised him up from his life as a shepherd boy to become the king of Israel. He had protected him during the storms and the wilderness wandering. He had given him victory over his enemies and the giants of his life. He had been merciful when David got it wrong and made mistakes. For David, that thankfulness overflowed in his worship, a pilgrimage into joy that defines so many of his songs.

That sense of joy wasn't a mere feeling of happiness, because surely that would fade away when the hard times came. It was a declaration that his reason to be thankful was beyond the circumstances of his life, but came instead from the God who held David in the palm of his hand. Notice that Psalm 100 gives the reason to be thankful as: 'the LORD is good and his love endures for ever'; not the fact that David has a lovely palace and a secure position.

It's interesting that the word 'gratitude' comes from the Latin word *gratia*, which means grace. The main reason for our gratitude as Christians is the grace that God has so freely poured out on us, grace that you can receive as a shepherd boy or as a king.

Also, notice that David is thankful for who he is before God. Not the king of Israel, but a sheep within the pasture of the Lord. If I think about my own life, there are many things to be thankful for. One of the things I am most thankful for is who I am before God, because it roots me, and humbles me, and encourages me – no matter the season of life that I find myself in. Paul says to the Corinthians: 'But by the grace of God I am what I am, and his grace to me was not without effect.'[14]

I am grateful for all that God has done to lead me to this point in my life, and I am grateful that he hasn't finished with me yet. I am grateful that he loves me without condition, and he loves me enough to take me further and deeper into him, and into the person he has created me to be.

David was a man who knew what it was to be thankful, and to let that thankfulness spill out into praise. For him and for us, cultivating a thankful heart is a lifelong pilgrimage, but one where every step, no matter how painful, can be looked back on to see the goodness of God.

Lament

Do you show your wonders to the dead?
    Do their spirits rise up and praise you?
Is your love declared in the grave,
    your faithfulness in Destruction?
Are your wonders known in the place of darkness,
    or your righteous deeds in the land of oblivion?

But I cry to you for help, LORD;
>   in the morning my prayer comes before you.
Why, LORD, do you reject me
>   and hide your face from me?
From my youth I have suffered and been close to death;
>   I have borne your terrors and am in despair.
Your wrath has swept over me;
>   your terrors have destroyed me.
All day long they surround me like a flood;
>   they have completely engulfed me.
You have taken from me friend and neighbour –
>   darkness is my closest friend.[15]

Over the past couple of years, I have had the pleasure of doing some teaching on a Master's degree course at Waverley Abbey, Surrey, looking at how we engage pastorally with suffering, both theologically and practically.

One of the things we talk about in those lectures, or whenever I go and speak on these issues, is Psalm 88.

What would it look like if someone was to pray this psalm in your church during a time of open prayer? What would your reaction be to hearing it?

So often, our assumption is that worship should be a joyful experience, and we fail to recognize that there are those who come to worship who are really struggling, for whom it has been a real and genuine battle just to get themselves through the door. In a chapter on the psalms of lament in my book *When Rain Falls Like Lead*, I explored some of this: 'We need to recognise that not everyone in our congregation will be in a place of lament, but perhaps we have failed to realize in recent times that not everyone is in a place of joy.'[16]

How do we engage with people in this place of lament? How can we offer a space of authenticity in worship, *both* for those for whom life is a struggle *and* for those for whom life is going well? That is a great challenge within our church culture, and one that we need to rise to, especially in these difficult times.

When it comes to the psalms of lament, I feel they are important for two key reasons.

1. They give us permission

The questions that these psalms raise, the doubts they express, and the honesty with which they offer these to us, give us permission not only to feel these emotions but also to express them as worship. If David could write these words and express them to God in worship, then perhaps it's OK for me, for us, to feel and express them too? I don't need to be 'happy clappy' all the time.

Psalm 88, unlike the others, doesn't have a resolution. There is no statement such as 'I will yet praise him'[17] that we get in other psalms of lament. Many of us can attest to being in this place. We know that, as Ian Stackhouse writes, 'this is exactly how it feels: God seems to have abandoned us. No matter how much we cry out there is no answer. No amount of arm twisting gets a response.'[18]

That sense of permission can also come when we look at how Jesus quotes the psalms of lament when on the cross. Those haunting words of deeply felt abandonment, 'Why have you forsaken me?', are also the words written by David many centuries before. Psalm 22 begins:

My God, my God, why have you forsaken me?

> Why are you so far from saving me,
> so far from my cries of anguish?[19]

So not only does the existence of these psalms give us a sense of permission to express similar feelings, but so too does the cry of Jesus on the cross; he also uses the Psalms as an expression of his lament.

And that leads me to the second reason why these psalms are important.

2. They help us to pray

Not only do the psalms of lament give me a sense of permission, but they also give me the words to pray when my own words fail me: 'When my prayers find the silence of heaven, and no words return, when my feeble attempts to articulate what is going on in my heart and soul fail time and time again, the words of the psalmist can speak for me.'[20]

There is something powerful in allowing the words of Scripture to speak for us. So often, we can read the Psalms and try to take from them some sort of academic truth about God, rather than using them as a means of connecting with God. Sometimes our own words come naturally, and at other times we need to use other people's words to give expression to the cries of our hearts. This is where the Psalms can help.

As a people of Scripture, and not just of the New Testament, this should encourage us. Theologian Claus Westermann, when discussing the psalms of lament, writes: 'I know of no text in the New Testament which would prevent the Christian from lamenting or would express the idea that faith in Christ excluded lamentation from a person's relation-ship with God.'[21]

Our spaces of worship, whether personal or shared with others, are places of safety and nurture where there is the free-dom to express both our joys and our sorrows.

Several years ago I went through a very painful time in my life and ministry. I was signed off work with depression; my working patterns and coping strategies, far from sustaining me, had become toxic and were causing a great deal of harm. As I touched on in a previous chapter, while I was signed off work, Bex and I went regularly to St Peter's in Brighton. It was exactly the kind of church that I would have loved to be in at any other time, but my experience there was very differ-ent from my normal experience of worship. It was a time of lament, not a time to dance. Worship for me during this time was expressed in tears. I would open my mouth to sing, but tears came instead. I would cry through most of the service, and then go forward for prayer at the end. This went on for the majority of the three months that we attended the church.

As painful as that time was, it also had beauty within it. It was honest, raw and without pretence.

David was a man who knew what it was to go through dark times. He knew too that he could take his doubts and ques-tions to the God who was bigger than his circumstances. He was a man comfortable with lament. In the dark and painful places of your life, let these psalms of David give you permis-sion, and also give you the words, to bring yourself into the presence of God. As John Goldingay says: 'The psalm as a whole is the Psalter's most extraordinary gift from God to the person whose experience makes him or her need to pray in this way.'[22]

Confession

> Have mercy on me, O God,
>> according to your unfailing love;
> according to your great compassion
>> blot out my transgressions.
> Wash away all my iniquity
>> and cleanse me from my sin.[23]

Something that as Christians we are all familiar with is confession. Within the Protestant tradition we have often shied away from it because of its prominence within the Catholic Church. However, it forms an important part of our worship life, both corporately and individually. American preacher and theologian Frederick Buechner writes: 'To confess your sins to God is not to tell him anything he doesn't already know. Until you confess them, however, they are the abyss between you. When you confess them, they become the bridge.'[24]

And right at the heart of confession is Psalm 51. This psalm gives us an insight into the man that David was. It also gives us an insight into the God whom David followed, which is significant. It is because God is a God of unfailing love and great compassion that David feels confident to bring his petition. Perhaps David already had in his heart and mind the words that would later form part of Psalm 103:

> The LORD is compassionate and gracious,
>> slow to anger, abounding in love.[25]

There are some who have suggested that David's plea to be made clean, for God to *wash away* his iniquity, is a reference to the ritualistic washing that was taking place as part of the worship at the temple in Jerusalem.[26] However, David's plea goes far deeper than ritual; his need is for washing to take place at a soul level:

> Create in me a pure heart, O God,
>   and renew a steadfast spirit within me.[27]

Why does it need such deep-level spirit surgery to set the problem right? Isn't saying 'sorry' enough?

The problem isn't so much with the actions, although David's actions in his affair with Bathsheba and his murder of Uriah were terribly destructive; the problem is what leads to the actions. It is the problem that sin caused when it first entered into the world and the human heart.

As the devil said to the first humans when they were enticed by the apple in the Garden of Eden: 'God knows that when you eat from it your eyes will be opened, and you will be like God . . .'[28] This lie was tempting us to put ourselves in the place of God. And, rather than letting God be at the centre of our worship, we placed ourselves there. Far from this making us like God, it has caused damage to our relationship with God, one another and creation in a dramatic way.

After his sins of adultery and murder, what David needed was a new heart. As Eugene Peterson reflects: 'Adoration of God had receded, and obsession with self had moved in.'[29] David was no longer worshipping God at that moment. He had replaced God at the centre of his life and worship, and instead was enjoying being king. He had bought the same lie the serpent had sold in the garden, and it had done terrible damage to his relationship with God, to Bathsheba and Uriah, and to his own heart. Only a heart transplant would do; only soul renewal could set him right.

We buy the same lie too. It is the lie that the serpent, the devil, the enemy has been peddling since the garden: 'Take back control, be your own master, do what makes you happy. Take your rightful place as captain of your own destiny.' It's an enticing piece of fruit, right?

And just as it is with anything you know you shouldn't eat, it's often only afterwards that the regret hits home. The response to that regret, to that shame, is to hide. That's what Adam and Eve did back in the garden: they hid from God. For us, too, as we come face to face with the state of our hearts, we can find the desire to hide from God and from others an appealing one. Why do we do this? Why is sin so often associated with shame? Partly because we realize that, despite the lie, we are not like God at all. We have put ourselves in that place, and we haven't measured up. We were never meant to. As my friend Ian says when reflecting on this psalm: 'Holiness is not the ability to pretend a perfect life but rather the willingness to face the residual darkness in our hearts, to bring it all before God, and then experience the renewing grace of the Holy Spirit.'[30]

Remember who it is that David addresses this psalm to: the God of unfailing love and great compassion, the one who will not despise a contrite spirit and a broken heart but who in his great mercy will wash us clean, making us whiter than snow, giving us a clean heart and a right spirit.

Confession is more than wandering into a booth, or a few quiet moments of reflection in a church service. It is the holding of who we are before God as an offering of worship. *This is me, Lord. You know my heart and you know it needs cleaning up; please make me new.*

As we pray that prayer, let's join with Pete Greig in remembering: 'There is more grace in God than sin in you.'[31]

Whole Life

As we draw this section of our journey to a close, how can we sum up David's heart of worship, and what lessons can we learn from him as we seek to reflect his heart for God?

The depth of the Psalms, both in terms of their beauty and expression, and also in terms of how much of life they cover, highlights to us that David was a man whose worship had a whole-life expression. This was no 'one-day-a-week' worshipper, but a man who lived out his faith in every area of his life. For a man who wrote so many songs, he knew that worship had to be lived out beyond the notes on a page.

We ask ourselves: what should my expression of worship be? What David had embraced was something that Paul would later go on to express to the Romans: 'So here's what I want you to do, God helping you: Take your everyday, ordinary life – your sleeping, eating, going-to-work, and walking-around life – and place it before God as an offering.'[32]

It's your whole life. It's all of you. You are the prayer, you are the song, you are the thanksgiving you offer, the lament you cry, the confession you plead – because it is born out of your whole life. Worship is not something you bring that is other than yourself; it is the bringing of yourself before the God who delights in your praises.

There are endless, creative ways to express that, as David knew, and like him we need to explore these both as churches and communities and as individuals. Let's get rid of this notion of worship as simply the songs we sing on a Sunday. Genuine worship is offered at great cost because it comes from within us, from the essence of who we are, and the fabric of our day-to-day lives. Is it a cost we are willing to pay? I hope so, and I pray for myself, and for you, that we might join with David in worship and say, 'I will not give to the Lord that which costs me nothing.'

Questions for Reflection

1. Worship is God-centred. How do we know we are actually worshipping God?

2. Do you long for God's presence in all areas of your life?

3. Would you describe your worship as extravagant? If not, what holds you back?

4. The psalms cover thanksgiving, lament and confession. Which elements do you find harder to bring into your worship?

5. What will going deeper in worship cost you? Are you willing to pay the price in response to God's love for you?

6. What does your pilgrimage journey look like?

7. What is your favourite psalm?

9

Going the Way of All the Earth

These are the last words of David:

'The inspired utterance of David son of Jesse,
    the utterance of the man exalted by the Most High,
the man anointed by the God of Jacob,
    the hero of Israel's songs . . .'[1]

At the age of 70, King David died. You might think that those simple words bring to a close the journey we have been taking together, but in fact it leaves us with one last exploration to make. Over the past eight chapters we have explored how David lived, and in this final chapter we will explore how David died. For even right at the end of David's life, there are lessons we can learn; practical lessons that will affect our lives and the lives of those around us.

Death and Taxes

Shortly after my own father died, a friend of the family wrote a book about his life called *Wholly Available*. At the end of the book she included the 'Christian Comment' from the local newspaper that had been written by him not long before he died. In it, he recalls meeting a man in his late twenties in the cardiac ward of the hospital. The young man was waiting for a heart transplant that could save his life, and eventually this is what he got. My father continued: 'But the transplant only postponed the inevitable, for death comes to us all sooner or later. Most pack a great deal into their lives; career, family holidays, just living. Yet they give virtually no thought to the only certainty in life – that it will end, and to what happens after death.'[2]

I wonder how many go through life like that? We often spend a great deal of time trying to distract ourselves from our own mortality. To some degree it is the great coping mechanism, because if we were to have to come face to face with the fragility of our own existence every day then it would be very difficult to truly live. I suggest that's totally right. I don't think it would do us any good at all to fixate on death, but neither do I think that it is healthy to avoid thought of it altogether.

A hundred and fifty years ago in Victorian Britain, the subject of sex was taboo and all anyone talked about was death. Fast-forward a century and a half, and life is quite the opposite: sex is everywhere and death is taboo.

We spend our hard-earned money to buy products that will reverse or mask the ageing process, we are fixated on fitness and diet, we want to live in the present moment – most of the time because we are trying to delay something that cannot be delayed.

The Bible certainly makes it clear that life does not go on forever.

When David's son Absalom sends for the wise woman from Tekoa, she tells him: 'Like water spilled on the ground, which cannot be recovered, so we must die.'[3]

According to the Teacher in Ecclesiastes, there is a time for everything under heaven, including 'a time to be born and a time to die'.[4]

The Scriptures do not shy away from the reality that we will all die. This is a fact that David, as he approaches the end of his life, is also aware of: 'When the time drew near for David to die, he gave a charge to Solomon his son. "I am about to go the way of all the earth," he said.'[5]

We will explore that passage a little more in a moment.

If death is something that comes to us all, or death is a journey we will all take, then surely it is better to prepare for that journey than to put it off. If we are going on a family holiday, we prepare to make the journey. We plan, we prepare, we make ready. We don't just wake up on the morning of the trip and rush to throw stuff into the car, because that is not a pleasant experience for anyone. Yet when it comes to the end of our lives, that is exactly what many people do. They spend years avoiding the reality that they will make this journey, and then spend a frantic last few moments chucking things into the suitcase trying to prepare.

However, if we can ready ourselves in advance, not knowing when the day might come, then we will find it a much smoother journey when we do leave. As Henri Nouwen says: 'I have a deep sense . . . that if we could really befriend death we would be free people.'[6] After all, unlike the family holiday, once we have left we cannot go back and get anything we forgot.

Having lost both my father and my sister at a young age, I have grown up thinking much more about issues to do with death than many people. My sister Hannah and I had organ donor cards from a very young age, and we talked openly about those things. That preparation was a huge blessing after she died, because I was able to go with her husband and speak to the organ donor nurse. It was not a pleasant experience to go through, but the one comfort I took in that process was that I knew what Hannah wanted – because she had prepared.

So how do we prepare ourselves?

Five Stages of Grief

First, we should acknowledge that dealing with death is a process. It is one thing to plan for something you know is going to happen at some point in the future, and something else to be faced with it up close and personal.

I worked for a year as a chaplain in St Christopher's Hospice in London, the first hospice in the UK. While I was there, I helped to support patients who were coming to the end of their lives. Some were in the hospice as day visitors, and others were there at the final stages of their lives. These individuals knew that they were part of a process, that they were on a journey and that they would feel different things at different times about what they were facing.

One of the most helpful internal maps for this journey came in the form of the Five Stages of Grief. This was a theory developed by psychiatrist Elisabeth Kübler-Ross in her work with patients facing death. She found, through speaking with patients and learning from them, that she could better understand how to care for them.

In her important book *On Death and Dying*, she spells out not only the importance of these five stages but also the importance of what she and other medical professionals have learned from those who are dying, understanding that people who are approaching the end of their lives have much to teach us.

I want us to look briefly at these stages, because I think they can help us as either we, or those we love, journey towards death. We may not be in that place at the moment, but as we have already admitted, all of us will make that journey in the end.

Stage one: denial

When a person is told that they are dying, sometimes it can be hard to accept, even more so if the person seems to be physically well. Over the years, I have journeyed with many people who have found it difficult to accept a terminal illness because they feel so well. They think, *Maybe the doctor was wrong? I'm still so young*. Denial can be an initial way of defending ourselves; our brains are very good at protecting us from information that is harmful to us.

When faced with a serious diagnosis, acceptance can be a hard position to find. I remember when I was in hospital and the doctor told me that I had growths on my brain. It was as if the world suddenly slowed down, and it was very hard to take the information on board. I sat at the end of my hospital bed thinking, *surely that can't be right*.

I remember the same feeling when my sister Hannah suffered her fatal stroke back in 2005. I got a phone call from my dad to explain to me what had happened, and I remember thinking, *surely that can't be right. She's 20 years old*.

Denial to some degree is an attempt to protect us from death. We are hardwired to cling to life and to flee from death, both physically and mentally. However, given the space and support to work through our thoughts and emotions, we can move to at least a partial acceptance.

Stage two: anger

Once we have reached that place where we can to some degree accept what is happening, sometimes we feel angry. Angry at the situation, perhaps angry with the doctors or medical staff, maybe even angry at God. Then we begin to ask the question: why me? In the second chapter of my first book *When Rain Falls Like Lead*, I talk about how the question 'why' is the most normal and immediate question when we come face to face with suffering. It feels as though the difficult things that happen to us are unfair, or we are caught up with thoughts of what we will miss out on, or worries and fears for the immediate future.

Kübler-Ross reminds us that 'this stage of anger is very difficult to cope with from the point of view of family and staff'[7] – namely the people with a responsibility to care for and support the person who is faced with death. One of the challenges with anger is that it is rarely focused. It fires off in all directions and can harm those whom the person experiencing the anger never intended to harm.

The quote I referred to in my previous chapter on conflict is relevant here again: 'If you don't heal what hurt you, then you'll bleed on those who didn't cut you.' In other words, if we are not careful, in our anger we will cause pain to those who simply want to care for and support us.

Perhaps you have been in that position, either as the person in pain or as the person on the receiving end of anger? In this situation, patience and love are key, for in many ways this is the most challenging stage for all involved.

Here it is easy for a person to feel a loss of hope because the emotion can be overwhelming, as Wendy Bray and Chris Ledger highlight in their book *Insight into Anger*: '[Anger] affects almost every area of our lives, impacting not just our emotions but our bodies and our mental and our spiritual health.'[8]

It is also important that we don't skip over this part of the process. God is big enough to hold our anger and our pain, and the healthiest thing we can do with it is to bring it to him, rather than feel as though we have to 'have it all together'.

Stage three: bargaining

In this stage a person may bargain for less pain, or more time with loved ones, or even a miraculous cure. It is again part of the way in which our brains protect us from the reality of the situation facing us, in an attempt to believe that it is not true.

In a situation where we are approaching death, sometimes we feel scared, vulnerable and helpless. We feel a lack of control over our own lives and even over life itself. All the things we have instinctively done over the years to take care of ourselves – looking both ways before we cross the street, eating well, exercising – were all measures of control designed to keep us safe and give us the longest life we could lead.

Now, at the moment we are told that death is approaching, there is nothing we are able to do. There is no measure we can take to make a difference.

Bargaining, to some degree, is an attempt to get that control back.

Some people may ask for other or additional medical opinions. Some people will want to try experimental treatments. Others might try to make a deal with God.

In *On Death and Dying* Kübler-Ross makes the comparison between this stage and the behaviour we sometimes see in our children. She highlights a well-known exchange: 'If I am very good all week and wash the dishes, will you let me go?'[9]

Bargaining is something we have always been used to, but at the end, when all control seems to have gone, it is what we often fall back into.

Again, when I think back to my sister's death, I remember this bargaining phase well. I was walking in the grounds of Salisbury District Hospital, and prayed one of the most heartfelt and honest prayers I have ever prayed. I said to God that if he could allow me to switch places with Hannah, then I would do it in a heartbeat. It was a desperate prayer. It was a bargaining prayer.

Stage four: depression

As we give ourselves time, and we work through the emotions that surround approaching death, what can come to us is a sense in which death is inevitable and will happen no matter what we do. The state that can develop at this moment is what Kübler-Ross describes as 'depression'.

Depression as a condition has been recognized since around 400 BC. It was called something different back then, *melancholia*, which included 'prolonged sadness and fear, with a decreased appetite and insomnia, sometimes with somatic symptoms such as gastrointestinal distress and suicidality'.[10]

The feelings we experience in these moments have existed long before there was a term for them, and they have long been associated with our preparations for dying.

This is where grief comes in. We start to feel a sense of sorrow that we will not be around to see the people we love journey through life. If death comes at a younger age, and we have families, then we will think about not seeing our children grow up. When I was faced with an uncertain future after the discovery of the growths on my brain, the thought that probably caused me most distress, in the darkness of a sleepless night, was the possibility, if it was a serious diagnosis, that I would not grow old with my wife, and that I might not get to watch my son grow up, to see him get married and be part of all that life held as a family.

Fortunately, my diagnosis was far better than that, but that is often where our minds and hearts go to when we are faced with death. As we will see in a moment, it is people and our relationships that really matter to us.

Kübler-Ross speaks about two types of depression in people dealing with approaching death: reactive and preparatory depression.[11]

Reactive depression is simply a depression that is in response to something that has already happened. Bereavement following the death of a loved one would fall into this category.

Preparatory depression, however, is the depression we experience as we approach an event that causes loss. This is the kind of depression which we, and our loved ones, experience as we approach death. In *On Death and Dying* we are reminded that it isn't helpful to try and 'cheer people up' when they are in this stage of depression. I know, as I'm sure many of you will too, the pain of losing a person that you love. However, 'the patient is in the process of losing everything and everybody they know'.[12]

As we approach death, the hope we can have of moving out of this stage and into acceptance can only come if we allow ourselves, or those we love and care for, to move through it.

Stage five: acceptance

Finally, there is acceptance. By this stage a person has already been through a great emotional journey, and one which hopefully, with support, will have made it possible for them to process what is happening to them.

Many in this final stage have an experience of peace and calm. However, Kübler-Ross rightly cautions us that acceptance does not necessarily mean happiness.

It is a stage where a person wants to die with dignity, and to allow this to be the last gift that they give to those around them.

Acceptance from a spiritual perspective is also significant because, as those who follow Jesus, we know that death is not the last word of the story, and the plans that God has for us don't finish at the grave. Acceptance here can take the form of hope – the firm belief that even for the person who faces death, it is not a hopeless end that they are destined for, but an endless hope.

It is important to think about these stages, because at least being aware of them will help us to be able to care for and support others as they go the way of all the earth, and help us to die well ourselves when our time comes. It is worth remembering at the same time that 'no two people are the same. Everyone reacts differently and at their own pace and many do not go through all the . . . stages.'[13]

What Really Matters – Relationships

As David's life comes to an end, he becomes more reflective. What is interesting is what he reflects on. In both 2 Samuel 23 and 1 Kings 2, passages that give us an insight into the end of David's life, what David focuses on is relationship. At the end of the day, that is what often matters most to us.

He thinks of those he leaves behind. He thinks of those who have stood by him. He thinks of those who have stood against him.

I will look a little later in the chapter at how David prepares Solomon for his death, and how we might prepare others, but for now I want to think about the other two categories I have mentioned: those who have stood with us and those who have stood against us.

1. Those who have stood with us

These are the names of David's mighty warriors:

Josheb-Basshebeth, a Tahkemonite, was chief of the Three; he raised his spear against eight hundred men, whom he killed in one encounter.

Next to him was Eleazar son of Dodai the Ahohite. As one of the three mighty warriors, he was with David when they taunted the Philistines gathered at Pas Dammim for battle. Then the Israelites retreated, but Eleazar stood his ground and struck down the Philistines till his hand grew tired and froze to the sword. The LORD brought about a great victory that day. The troops returned to Eleazar, but only to strip the dead.

Next to him was Shammah son of Agee the Hararite. When the Philistines banded together at a place where there was a field full of lentils, Israel's troops fled from them. But Shammah took his stand in the middle of the field. He defended it and struck the Philistines down, and the LORD brought about a great victory.[14]

Why is it that David included these men in his last words? Perhaps it is because they were the ones who stood with him during the most difficult and challenging moments of his life. By any measure that matters, these were some of the most important people in David's life.

In my book *Made to Belong*,[15] I mentioned that the well-quoted saying, 'Blood is thicker than water,' actually comes from a fuller quote: 'The blood of the covenant is thicker than the water of the womb.' The original meaning was that the blood shed by soldiers together on the battlefield gives birth to a relationship that is often deeper than that of biological families. Or as Shakespeare's King Henry V put it before the battle of Agincourt:

For he to-day that sheds his blood with me
Shall be my brother . . .[16]

These men were David's brothers. They might not have shared the same blood, but they had shed that blood in many battlefields across the land. They had risked their lives for him and so had found a special place not just in the pages of his history, but also written into the very fabric of his heart. Ian Coffey, reflecting on why these names are included in Scripture, notes that in part it was because David wanted them to be included: 'When the records were being written he wanted to remember his friends. And there is much we can learn from that simple gesture of loyalty.'[17]

Who makes it on to the pages of your history? Who have you written there? Perhaps when faced with these men and their relationship to David the question should be: who have you written into the fabric of your heart? And do they know it?

As we prepare to face death, there is one fact that can throw our thinking out of line and rob us of preparing well: many of us do not know when the day of our death will be. If I knew that I would die exactly one year from today, I would plan. I would decide what I wanted to do with the time that I had left, I would put right the wrongs and broken relationships, and I would make sure that those I loved knew that I loved them. If I knew the day . . . but we don't. What we do know, though, is that the day is coming. It might be a year from now; it might be fifty years from now; it might be tomorrow. The fact that we don't know the exact moment of our deaths is not a reason to abandon planning; it is all the more reason to plan, and to do it now! Johann Christoph Arnold asks us: 'Do we cherish each other? Do we realize that every encounter might be our last chance to show our love?'[18]

So, have I told the people whom I love that I love them? Because I don't want them to be in any doubt. When my sister Hannah died unexpectedly in 2005, one of the comforts we had as a family is that we knew that we had not left anything unsaid. Of course we were heartbroken that we would not have the opportunity to say those things to her again in this life, but we knew that she knew we loved her, and we knew that she loved us. Her name was written on to our hearts, and our names were written on to hers.

Is that true for your loved ones today? In fact, why not make this a lesson you can learn from King David today. Take a moment today to do some heart writing; to let those you love know that you love them and value them.

They might be family in the biological sense, or they might be, like Josheb-Basshebeth, Eleazar and Shammah, those who have shed their blood with you in the battlefields of life.

Make sure they know. It is a key preparation before going the way of all the earth.

2. Those who have stood against us

> Now you yourself know what Joab son of Zeruiah did to me – what he did to the two commanders of Israel's armies, Abner son of Ner and Amasa son of Jether. He killed them, shedding their blood in peacetime as if in battle, and with that blood he stained the belt around his waist and the sandals on his feet. Deal with him according to your wisdom, but do not let his grey head go down to the grave in peace.[19]

There are regrets. And most of the regrets we have centre on relationships – on those we have wronged, and those who have wronged us. This passage of Scripture is a complicated one for us in many ways. David is asking Solomon to settle accounts in a way that he himself wasn't able to.

There are a couple of lessons we can learn here from David, both in something he fails to do, and in something I would encourage us not to emulate. We can learn from David not only when he does well but also when he does badly.

What we can see in this short passage, and as the account unfolds in 1 Kings 2, is that once again when faced with death, David's mind is on relationships. In many ways it is far easier to do what we have just been exploring: to speak words of love and affirmation to those close to us. What do we do, though, when the relationship is complicated? What do we do when the relationship has been broken?

Begin with prayer. If our heart's desire is to see relationship restored, as much as it can be, then we can begin by simply praying for three things.

First, that God would open our heart in love to the other person and bless them.

Second, that God would open their heart to us.

Third, that God would give us the opportunity to take steps towards restoration, and give us the courage to take them.

I am not saying that by praying these three things, all relationships will be miraculously healed. We are complex people, and wherever relationships are complex, sometimes the healing will take time. However, what these prayers create or reveal is an intention in our hearts towards restoration. That is an intention that is missing in what David shares with Solomon here on his deathbed. Pain and bitterness are still present, and so is the desire for vengeance.

It is that vengeance, that desire to settle a score, or at the least, the unwillingness to bring healing to a relationship that is what I would encourage us not to emulate in David.

We saw in an earlier chapter how David dealt with conflict well, but as we approach the end of our lives relationships can become challenging, and our capacity is reduced. It is far better to not let it get to this stage, and to deal with our broken relationships before we come to the end of our lives.

What David does here is to pass his feuds on to Solomon. I have seen this in families, where the grudges of the parents are passed on and upheld by the children, precisely because the relationship wasn't healed before the parents died. It might not reach the level of David's words: 'Do not let his grey head go down to the grave in peace,' but it still has an impact on the generations to come.

Part of the reason for seeking to heal those relationships is precisely so that the conflict will die before we do, and we will not pass it on to the next generation. Look at it on a national scale – in sectarian conflicts in Ireland and the Middle East. One generation passes on the conflict to another, and so the circle of brokenness continues, because nobody has wanted healing more than to 'be on the right side'. That is probably a gross oversimplification of very complex national issues, but eventually there will be generations who long to die in peace, and long for their children to live in peace, more than they want to win the argument.

Don't pass your broken relationships on. A way to do that is to seek to bring healing, or make amends before you go the way of all the earth.

'My Son . . .'

When the time drew near for David to die, he gave a charge to Solomon his son.

'I am about to go the way of all the earth,' he said. 'So be strong, act like a man, and observe what the LORD your God requires: walk in obedience to him, and keep his decrees and commands, his laws and regulations, as written in the Law of Moses. Do this so that you may prosper in all you do and wherever you go and that the LORD may keep his promise to me: "If your descendants watch how they live, and if they walk faithfully before me with all their heart and soul, you will never fail to have a successor on the throne of Israel."'[20]

Here we come across a beautiful scene where David is preparing Solomon for his death. David knows that his death will be significant, and he knows that the pressure will be on Solomon. So he wants to make sure that Solomon is prepared for life without him and all that this will mean. The advice is personal at times, it is professional (monarch to heir), and it is specific. It is because he loves his son that David wants to make sure he is prepared for what is to come.

As we too think about dying, as we think about how one day we will also go the way of all the earth, we need to think about how we can prepare those around us for the time when we will no longer be here. None of us likes to think of leaving grieving loved ones behind, but I can tell you this: in almost two decades of pastoral ministry, the big difference in the families of those I visit is between those who have prepared and those who haven't. I can also tell you that there is a great deal of distress for many bereaved people when they get to that moment, when they realize that they have no idea what their loved one's wishes were.

Henri Nouwen summed this up when he said: 'When we think of death, we often think about what will happen to us after we have died. But it is more important to think about what will happen to those we leave behind.'[21]

Several years ago I ran an evening 'café church' event in Bath, which I called 'Going the Way of All the Earth'. It was an event with the express purpose of getting people to think about how to prepare for death. We began by asking people to write their own epitaph, and then in smaller groups we went on to explore the things that we could do to prepare for death. I'm including some of these things below to help us think through some of the more practical preparations.

Write a will

This is one of the most helpful ways in which we can prepare practically. It will be a blessing to those we leave behind to know what our wishes are. Wills are fairly straightforward to put together. You can even get ready-made kits in certain shops on the high street, or you can book an appointment to speak to a solicitor. When you have made a will, make sure that those you love know that you have done it, and who holds that will, so that they can make arrangements after your death.

Two heads are better than one

Over the years, I have met pastorally with many different people in preparing for death. One of the difficult practical issues is when one partner has 'taken charge' of a particular area of the couple's life, and the other has no idea how to manage now that the person has either gone or is about to die. For example, it may be that one of the two takes care of the finances; he or she is then the only one who has access to the bank accounts, knows the online passwords, and so on. There are ways to get through this after a person has died, but it is much easier if there has been a conversation so that the other partner knows where things are, and how to manage them, before the other dies.

It might be that one person deals with all the utility bills, which means the other may not know which company supplies their gas and electricity, or phone lines, and such like. Perhaps in this situation it would be good to have noted down, somewhere secure, all those details so that both of you know, when the time comes, where the other can find that information.

Plan a funeral

I recently visited a neighbour following the unexpected death of her husband. She told me that they had never spoken about their wishes for their funerals – until a week before he passed away. She was so grateful that this conversation had come up, because neither of them was to know that within a week he would be dead. Your own funeral may seem a strange thing to think about, especially if you are young and seemingly fit and healthy, but again it is an important thing to do. Even if you feel that this is not something you want to discuss with others, it might be a good idea to put some thoughts down on paper and then let someone know where they are, so that when the times comes they are ready. What are your favourite hymns/songs; readings from Scripture; poems? Who would you like to take the service? Would you prefer to be buried or cremated; and where? Giving thought to these questions means that your loved ones can have confidence after your death, knowing that the service they put together is something you would not only be happy with, but have been part of preparing too.

Jesus Prepares Those He Loves

So David prepares those he loves for his death. Perhaps this is one of the most profound life lessons we can learn from him, because we too will one day join him on his journey.

It is also significant to see in the gospels that Jesus too prepares those he loves for his own death.

If you knew you were going to die tomorrow, how would you spend your last day? For me, the answer is: I would spend it with the people that I love most in all the world. I imagine that it would be the same for most of us. It was the same for Jesus too. That last evening before his death, he spends it with his friends, teaching them and preparing them for what is to come. John gives six chapters of his gospel to this preparation, which begins in chapter 13 with the Last Supper, and goes through to chapter 18 when Jesus and his friends cross the Kidron Valley and go up the Mount of Olives.

Jesus, too, knew he was going the way of all the earth. John tells us at the start of chapter 13: 'It was just before the Passover Festival. Jesus knew that the hour had come for him to leave this world and go to the Father. Having loved his own who were in the world, he loved them to the end.'[22]

Knowing that his death was approaching, Jesus chose to love. Preparing well for our death, both ourselves and others, is deeply pastoral and deeply loving. It is not simply about practicalities, but about relationship.

As Jesus continues, he speaks to his disciples more openly: 'In a little while you will see me no more, and then after a little while you will see me.'[23] He is not simply preparing them for his absence but also preparing them for the emotions that grief brings with it: 'Very truly I tell you, you will weep and mourn while the world rejoices. You will grieve, but your grief will turn to joy.'[24]

Jesus not only informs his friends of their grief, but there is a sense in which he also gives them permission to grieve. Even though he has told them that the Son of Man will rise again on the third day, he still knows that they will mourn and weep. In the same way, it is perfectly normal, acceptable and healthy for us to mourn the loss of a loved one, even though we have the hope of eternal life. Jesus didn't prepare the disciples for his death so that they wouldn't react to that painful loss when it came. He explains at the end of John 16 why he is preparing them: 'I have told you these things, so that in me you may have peace.'[25]

In the same way, when we prepare others for our death, we do not do so in order that they won't experience grief and loss when the times comes, but so that even as they approach that time, and when it arrives, they might have peace.

Jesus Prepares Himself for What Is to Come

Jesus went out as usual to the Mount of Olives, and his disciples followed him. On reaching the place, he said to them, 'Pray that you will not fall into temptation.' He withdrew about a stone's throw beyond them, knelt down and prayed, 'Father, if you are willing, take this cup from me; yet not my will, but yours be done.' An angel from heaven appeared to him and strengthened him. And being in anguish, he prayed more earnestly, and his sweat was like drops of blood falling to the ground.[26]

Until we reach the end of our lives, it is very difficult for us to comprehend what that moment is like. The five stages we looked at earlier give us a glimpse into that, and so does this short passage with Jesus in prayer in the Garden of Gethsemane. The name Gethsemane means 'pressing', and that is exactly what is happening here to Jesus. It feels as though he is being crushed by the anticipation of what is coming. This is preparatory depression.

Preparing for this moment prayerfully and honestly before God is so important.

Jesus does not hold anything back from the Father. He is anguished. He asks if there is any other way. Yet these prayers are offered to God in the holiness of the garden.

We too need to hold the complex and painful emotions of death and loss before God, honestly and prayerfully. We too in those moments can find strength to face what comes.

Jesus enters the garden with all the disciples, except Judas; he then goes a little deeper with Peter, James and John; and then he goes deeper still on his own to be with the Father.

In the moments when we prayerfully and honestly prepare for the end of life, there are places where it is appropriate and necessary to let a wider group of people in. There are also moments when it is appropriate and necessary to let a smaller, more intimate number in. Equally, there are moments when it is appropriate and necessary to hold, in the holy solitude of our prayerful hearts, the space that is just for us and the Father alone.

What we can learn from Jesus, and from David, as well as the work of healthcare professionals such as Elisabeth Kübler-Ross, is that preparing for death is a significant part of life. Perhaps it is the most significant of life lessons.

The need to prepare to take that journey, to go the way of all the earth, is important, and we will have different approaches to it depending on our age and background.

I have a good friend in my church, John, who is 95 years old. He said to me over coffee recently, as we were talking about this very issue, that he would be content to go home, have a sandwich, sit down in his chair, and then go to be with Jesus and those he loved in heaven. However, in my late thirties, I would be far less happy for that to happen to me.

If I think of my son, who is only young, even having this conversation with him would be a challenge to navigate.

We approach death differently depending on our stage of life, but the need to prepare for it is still as significant.

Over lunch, I was discussing this chapter with another friend, who is a retired pastor. He said to me that when he was a pastor, he had the painful task of taking the funeral of a 12-year-old girl. At what age do you begin to prepare people for death?

We began this chapter by stating that death is an inevitable part of life. We cannot escape it. And if we cannot escape it, then it will pop into our lives from time to time: through the death of a family member, or a pet, or in the news. Perhaps, when that happens, we have a natural opportunity to speak about these things in an age-appropriate way. The conversation then is not forced, but responsive and rooted in the rhythm of life.

Earlier this year there was a death in the staff team at my son's school. The death was very sudden and unexpected and it left the school community, especially the members of staff, very much in shock. The head teacher of the school went round to every class, read the pupils a book which aims to help children think about death, and then talked and listened to them. She did this with every class. It was responsive, un-forced, deeply pastoral and loving.

The deputy head, along with other staff, took the children whose teacher had died from the class, and they went for a walk in the local woods to give them space to think and share, and be together out of the classroom. For all these children it was a gift, because it helped them to begin to understand what we all must understand: the life lesson from King David – that one day we too will go the way of all the earth.

Keep Hold of Your Spoon

My friend John mentioned something important over our coffee, as he so often does: heaven.

The reason I have chosen in this chapter not to focus on what happens after we die is because I think the life lesson to learn here from David is much more about how we prepare for death rather than what follows it. However, as a Christian, how can you separate the two? Part of my preparing for the reality that one day this life will end is the hope that life in all its depth and vibrancy will carry on into eternity. I know that I was not made simply for this life, but I was made to be in the presence of God, to enjoy him and be enjoyed by him, when time itself will slip away.

In Colossians chapter 1, Paul writes some of the most stunning words of the New Testament: 'For God was pleased to have all his fullness dwell in [Jesus], and through him to reconcile to himself all things, whether things on earth or things in heaven, by making peace through his blood, shed on the cross.'[27]

The great redeeming work of the cross doesn't just draw humanity to a restored relationship with God and a brighter future. It draws *all creation* – things in heaven and on earth. As *The Message* puts it: 'people and things, animals and atoms'.

The way of all the earth is not simply death and decay, a destiny on the cosmic scrapheap or bonfire. It is life. Life is the goal, the destination towards which all things are moving. Death itself is either a totally defeated enemy or it is not defeated. Ultimately, in Jesus, the way of all the earth is restoration, is life. Yes, we must pass through death, as even Jesus himself did, but it is just a gateway, a passageway into the light.

This is the flow we are caught up in, the movement of the cosmos from the very beginning: to move into life, the life of the Father, Son and Holy Spirit.

To prepare for death is to prepare for life. To think of the ending of this life is to prepare for the beginning of the next.

Several years ago I took the funeral of a woman in our church who loved to bake, and I came across this story. It was of a woman who, when she knew that death was approaching, asked if she could be buried with a spoon in her hand. Her pastor was confused, and asked for the reason. She explained, 'When I used to go to the church lunches, when the main course was finished someone would always say "Keep hold of your spoon, because there's something else coming." So I want to be buried with a spoon in my hand, because I know that there is something else coming.'

As many people approach the end of their lives, they feel as though they are staring death in the face. However, because of Jesus, should we not be saying that what we are really staring in the face is life?

Questions for Reflection

1. Is your death something you have thought about much?

2. Who would you discuss this with?

3. If you are working through the pain of grief, where are you in the five stages? In denial, anger, bargaining, depression or acceptance?

4. As David nears death, he remembers those who stood by him. Whose names are written into your heart? Do they know that?

5. How can we make sure that we reach our end without unresolved bitterness from broken relationships?

6. In what practical ways can you help those you love prepare for your death?

7. Do you believe that preparing for death is actually preparing for life?

Notes

Introduction

1 1 Sam. 13:14; Acts 13:22.
2 Stephen Cherry, *Barefoot Disciple: Walking the Way of Passionate Humility* (London: Continuum, 2011), p. 13.
3 David Wolpe, *David: The Divided Heart* (London and New Haven, CT: Yale University Press, 2014), p. 125.
4 Heb. 11:33–34 NRSV.
5 Heb. 12:1 NRSV.
6 Matt. 3:17.
7 Archbishop Justin Welby, 'sermon for the State Funeral of Her Majesty Queen Elizabeth II', (2022) https://www.archbishopofcanterbury.org/speaking-writing/sermons/archbishop-canterburys-sermon-state-funeral-her-majesty-queen-elizabeth-ii (accessed 28 Sept. 2022).

1. The Secret Anointing

1 1 Sam. 9:2b NRSV.
2 1 Sam. 16:1–13 NRSV.
3 See Eugene Peterson, *The Message of David: Earthy Spirituality for Everyday Christians* (London: Marshall Pickering, 1997), p. 16.

4 Robert Alter, *The Hebrew Bible: A Translation with Commentary* (London: W.W. Norton, 2019), p. 241.

5 1 Sam. 16:11 NRSV.

6 1 Cor. 1:27.

7 Deut. 8:11–18 NRSV.

8 Zech. 4:6.

9 Shane Claiborne and Chris Haw, *Jesus for President: Politics for Ordinary Radicals* (Grand Rapids, MI: Zondervan, 2008), p. 47.

10 Matt. 4:18–22 NRSV.

11 Matt. 9:9 NRSV.

12 Shane Claiborne, *The Irresistible Revolution: Living as an Ordinary Radical* (Grand Rapids, MI: Zondervan, 2006), p. 245.

13 Peterson, *The Message of David*, p. 18.

14 Ps. 51:10 NRSV.

15 1 Sam. 16:7 NRSV.

16 Alter, *The Hebrew Bible*, p. 241.

17 Ps. 139:1–6.

18 Taken from *Facing Your Giants* by Max Lucado, p. 7. Copyright © 2006 by Max Lucado. Used by permission of HarperCollins Christian Publishing. www.harpercollinschristian.com.

2. Facing Your Giant

1 1 Sam. 17:1–11.

2 1 Sam. 17:26.

3 See David Wolpe, *David: The Divided Heart* (London and New Haven, CT: Yale University Press, 2014).

4 1 Sam. 17:45–47.

5 1 Sam. 17:11.

6 Ian Coffey, *The Story of David: After God's Heart* (Milton Keynes: Authentic, 2003), p. 14.

7 See 1 Sam. 17:26.

8 Prov. 27:17.

9   1 Sam. 17:34–37.

10   2 Sam. 21:15–17.

11   See Robert Alter, *The Hebrew Bible: A Translation with Commentary* (New York, NY: W.W. Norton, 2019), p. 406.

12   1 Sam. 17:38–40.

13   1 Sam. 17:48–50.

14   1 Sam. 17:45.

15   1 Cor. 15:57–58.

16   Rom. 8:31.

17   Rom. 8:37–39.

18   1 Sam. 17:32.

19   1 Sam. 17:47 (my emphasis).

20   Taken from *Facing Your Giants* by Max Lucado, p. 8. Copyright © 2006 by Max Lucado. Used by permission of HarperCollins Christian Publishing. www.harpercollinschristian.com.

3. Conflict

1   1 Chr. 22:8 NRSV.

2   Charles L. Whitfield, *Wisdom to Know the Difference: Core Issues in Relationships, Recovery and Living* (Atlanta, GA: Muse House Press, 2012), p. 87.

3   1 Sam. 18:6–9.

4   See Ben Dattner, *The Blame Game: How the Hidden Rules of Credit and Blame Determine Our Success or Failure* (New York, NY: Free Press, 2011), pp. 50–56.

5   Dattner, *The Blame Game*, p. 50.

6   1 Sam. 18:29.

7   Ian Coffey, *The Story of David: After God's Heart* (Milton Keynes: Authentic, 2003), p. 36.

8   1 Sam. 19:1a.

9   1 Sam. 20:2.

10   1 Sam. 18:3–4.

11   See 1 Sam. 14.

12 1 Sam. 20:42.

13 Eugene Peterson, *The Message of David: Earthy Spirituality for Everyday Christians* (London: Marshall Pickering, 1997), p. 53.

14 1 Sam. 18:12–13a.

15 1 Sam. 24:1–7.

16 Danny Silk, *Culture of Honor: Sustaining a Supernatural Environment* (Shippensburg, PA: Destiny Image, 2009), p. 161.

17 Bill T. Arnold, *1 & 2 Samuel*, NIV Application Commentary (Grand Rapids, MI: Zondervan, 2003), pp. 331–2.

18 Gen. 1:27 NRSV.

19 Gen. 2:7, translation by Robert Alter, *The Hebrew Bible: A Translation with Commentary* (New York, NY: W.W. Norton, 2019), p. 14.

20 Matt. 18:15–17.

21 William Barclay, *The Gospel of Matthew, Volume 2*, Daily Study Bible (Edinburgh: Saint Andrew Press, 1975), p. 188.

22 Prov. 27:6.

23 Matt. 18:17.

24 See Barclay, *The Gospel of Matthew, Vol. 2*, p. 187.

25 John 18:36.

4. The Waiting Game

1 See 2 Sam. 5:4.

2 See Scott Nelson, 'Average Credit Card Debt UK – Complete Analysis 2022', *MoneyNerd* (2022) https://moneynerd.co.uk/average-credit-card-debt (accessed 3 Aug. 2022).

3 See Chris Lilly, 'UK Credit Card Statistics: How Are Brits Using Their Credit Cards?' *Finder* (2022) www.finder.com/uk/credit-card-statistics (accessed 3 Aug. 2022).

4 Andy Percey, *Infused with Life: Exploring God's Gift of Rest in a World of Busyness* (Milton Keynes: Authentic, 2019).

5 Gen. 18:10–12.

6 Matt. 3:16–17.

7 Phil. 1:4–6.
8 Ps. 27:14.
9 Ps. 46:10.
10 See Robert Alter, *The Hebrew Bible: A Translation with Commentary* (New York, NY: W.W. Norton, 2019), p. 123.
11 2 Sam. 23:14–17.
12 Gal. 4:4.

5. Finding Common Ground

1 2 Sam. 5:1–5.
2 2 Sam. 5:6–10.
3 Article 1 of the Rights of Man and the Citizens, adopted on 26 August 1789 by the National Constituent Assembly of France.
4 The United States of America Declaration of Independence, signed on 4 July 1776 by the United States Congress.
5 Article 1 of the United Nations Declaration of Human Rights, proclaimed on 10 December 1948 by the General Assembly of the United Nations.
6 Gen. 1:27.
7 Col. 1:15–18 (my emphasis).
8 Eph. 4:1–6 (my emphasis).
9 John 17:20–21.
10 Ps. 133:1.
11 Isa. 43:18–19.
12 Rev. 21:5 NRSV.

6. Mephibosheth

1 2 Sam. 9:1–3.
2 2 Sam. 3:1.

3 Eugene Peterson, *The Message of David: Earthy Spirituality for Everyday Christians* (London: Marshall Pickering, 1997), p. 173.
4 Rom. 8:38–39.
5 1 John 4:10.
6 2 Sam. 9:4.
7 R.T. Kendall, *A Man after God's Own Heart: God's Relationship with David – and with You* (Fearn: Christian Focus, 2001), p. 246.
8 2 Sam. 9:8.
9 John Powell, *Why Am I Afraid to Love?* (Chicago, IL: Argus Communications, 1967), p. 29.
10 Gen. 16:7–10, 13.
11 Ps. 139:7–12.
12 2 Sam. 9:6.
13 John 20:16.
14 Isa. 43:1.
15 2 Sam. 9:7a.
16 Peterson, *The Message of David*, p. 171.
17 Rom. 8:1.
18 Heb. 4:16.
19 Rom. 8:31b.
20 2 Sam. 9:7b.
21 Taken from *Facing Your Giants* by Max Lucado, p. 125. Copyright © 2006 by Max Lucado. Used by permission of HarperCollins Christian Publishing. www.harpercollinschristian.com.
22 2 Sam. 9:11b.
23 1 John 3:1.
24 Philip Yancey, *What's So Amazing about Grace?* (Grand Rapids, MI: Zondervan, 1997), p. 171.
25 Matt. 25:40.
26 Luke 14:12–14.

7. Balcony Choices

1   2 Sam. 11:1–5.
2   The phrase 'David remained in Jerusalem' can literally be translated as 'David was *sitting* in Jerusalem'.
3   1 Sam. 8:19b–20.
4   Taken from *Facing Your Giants* by Max Lucado, p. 133. Copyright © 2006 by Max Lucado. Used by permission of HarperCollins Christian Publishing. www.harpercollinschristian.com.
5   R.T. Kendall, *A Man after God's Own Heart: God's Relationship with David – and with You* (Fearn: Christian Focus, 2001), p. 258.
6   Phil. 2:6–8.
7   2 Sam. 11:3.
8   2 Sam. 11:14–17.
9   John 10:10.
10 Deut. 30:19–20.
11 Ps. 51:1–10.
12 Ps. 51:11.
13 2 Tim. 2:13.

8. 'I Will Not Give to the Lord That Which Has Cost Me Nothing'

1   2 Sam. 24:18–25.
2   2 Sam. 6:14 NRSV.
3   2 Sam. 6:16 NRSV.
4   Matt Redman, 'Holy, Holy, Holy', *Premier Christianity* magazine, February 2021, p. 44, premierchristianity.com.
5   2 Sam. 6:13.
6   2 Sam. 6:19.

7 Oswald Chambers, *My Utmost for His Highest* (Carnforth: Discovery House, 2014), p. 58.
8 Pete Greig, *How to Pray: A Simple Guide for Normal People* (London: Hodder & Stoughton, 2019), p. 53.
9 Luke 6:45.
10 2 Sam. 6:16.
11 2 Sam. 6:20.
12 Ps. 100:1–5.
13 Ian Stackhouse, *Praying the Psalms: A Personal Journey through the Psalter* (Eugene, OR: Cascade, 2018), p. 104.
14 1 Cor. 15:10a.
15 Ps. 88:10–18.
16 Andy Percey, *When Rain Falls Like Lead: Exploring the Presence of God in the Darkness of Suffering* (Milton Keynes: Paternoster, 2013), p. 45.
17 Ps. 42:11.
18 Stackhouse, *Praying the Psalms*, p. 91.
19 Ps. 22:1.
20 Percey, *When Rain Falls Like Lead*, p. 53.
21 Claus Westermann, *Praise and Lament in the Psalms* (Atlanta, GA: John Knox Press, 1981), p. 264.
22 John Goldingay, *Psalms for Everyone, Part 2: Psalms 73–150* (London: SPCK, 2014), p. 58.
23 Ps. 51:1–2.
24 Frederick Buechner, *Wishful Thinking: A Theological ABC* (London: HarperCollins, 1987), p. 1.
25 Ps. 103:8.
26 See Gerald H. Wilson, *Psalms, Volume 1*, NIV Application Commentary (Grand Rapids, MI: Zondervan, 2002), pp. 773–4.
27 Ps. 51:10.
28 Gen. 3:5a.
29 Eugene Peterson, *The Message of David: Earthy Spirituality for Everyday Christians* (London: Marshall Pickering, 1997), p. 187.
30 Stackhouse, *Praying the Psalms*, p. 53.

31 Greig, *How to Pray*, p. 157.
32 Rom. 12:1 MSG.

9. Going the Way of All the Earth

1 2 Sam. 23:1.
2 Kitty Hay, *Wholly Available: The Story of David Ferneyhough* (Andover: self-published), p. 45.
3 2 Sam. 14:14a.
4 Eccl. 3:2.
5 1 Kgs 2:1–2a.
6 Henri Nouwen, *The Dance of Life: Spiritual Direction with Henri Nouwen*, ed. Michael Ford (London: Darton, Longman & Todd, 2005), p. 110.
7 Elisabeth Kübler-Ross, *On Death and Dying* (London: Tavistock, 1970), p. 44.
8 Wendy Bray and Chris Ledger, *Insight into Anger* (Farnham: CWR, 2007), p. 61.
9 Kübler-Ross, *On Death and Dying*, p. 72.
10 Charles L. Whitfield, *The Truth about Depression: Choices for Healing* (Deerfield Beach, FL: Health Communications, 2003), p. 9.
11 See Kübler-Ross, *On Death and Dying*, pp. 76–7.
12 Kübler-Ross, *On Death and Dying*, p. 77.
13 Stewart Matthew and Ken Lawson, *Caring for God's People: A Handbook for Elders and Ministers on Pastoral Care* (Edinburgh: Saint Andrew Press, 1995), p. 63.
14 2 Sam. 23:8–12.
15 Andy Percey, *Made to Belong: Moving beyond Tribalism to Find Our True Connection in God* (Milton Keynes: Authentic, 2021), p. 54.
16 William Shakespeare, *Henry V*, Act 4, Scene 3.
17 Ian Coffey, *The Story of David: After God's Heart* (Milton Keynes: Authentic, 2003), p. 207.

18 Johann Christoph Arnold, *I Tell You a Mystery: Life, Death and Eternity* (Robertsbridge: Plough Publishing House, 1996), p. 64.

19 1 Kgs 2:5–6.

20 1 Kgs 2:1–4.

21 Nouwen, *The Dance of Life*, p. 113.

22 John 13:1.

23 John 16:16.

24 John 16:20.

25 John 16:33a.

26 Luke 22:39–44.

27 Col. 1:19–20.

Bibliography

Alter, Robert. *The Hebrew Bible: A Translation with Commentary* (New York, NY: W.W. Norton, 2019).

Arnold, Bill T. *1 & 2 Samuel*, NIV Application Commentary (Grand Rapids, MI: Zondervan, 2003).

Arnold, Johann Christoph. *I Tell You a Mystery: Life, Death and Eternity* (Robertsbridge: Plough Publishing House, 1996).

Barclay, William. *The Gospel of Matthew, Volume 2*, Daily Study Bible (Edinburgh: Saint Andrew Press, 1975).

Bray, Wendy, and Chris Ledger. *Insight into Anger* (Farnham: CWR, 2007).

Buechner, Frederick. *Wishful Thinking: A Theological ABC* (London: HarperCollins, 1987).

Chambers, Oswald. *My Utmost for His Highest* (Carnforth: Discovery House, 2014).

Cherry, Stephen. *Barefoot Disciple: Walking the Way of Passionate Humility* (London: Continuum, 2011).

Claiborne, Shane. *The Irresistible Revolution: Living as an Ordinary Radical* (Grand Rapids, MI: Zondervan, 2006).

Claiborne, Shane, and Chris Haw. *Jesus for President: Politics for Ordinary Radicals* (Grand Rapids, MI: Zondervan, 2008).

Coffey, Ian. *The Story of David: After God's Heart* (Milton Keynes: Authentic, 2003).

Dattner, Ben. *The Blame Game: How the Hidden Rules of Credit and Blame Determine our Success or Failure* (New York, NY: Free Press, 2011).

Goldingay, John. *Psalms for Everyone, Part 2: Psalms 73–150* (London: SPCK, 2014).

Greig, Pete. *How to Pray: A Simple Guide for Normal People* (London: Hodder & Stoughton, 2019).

Hay, Kitty. *Wholly Available: The Story of David Ferneyhough* (Andover: self-published).

Kendall, R.T. *A Man after God's Own Heart: God's Relationship with David – and with You* (Fearn: Christian Focus, 2001).

Kübler-Ross, Elisabeth. *On Death and Dying* (London: Tavistock, 1970).

Lilly, Chris. 'UK Credit Card Statistics: How Are Brits Using Their Credit Cards?' *Finder* (2022) www.finder.com/uk/credit-card-statistics (accessed 3 August 2022).

Lucado, Max. *Facing Your Giants* (Nashville, TN: W Publishing Group, 2006).

Matthew, Stewart, and Ken Lawson. *Caring for God's People: A Handbook for Elders and Ministers on Pastoral Care* (Edinburgh: Saint Andrew Press, 1995).

McManus, Erwin Raphael. *The Way of the Warrior: An Ancient Path to Inner Peace* (New York, NY: Waterbrook, 2019).

Nelson, Scott. 'Average Credit Card Debt UK – Complete Analysis 2022'. *MoneyNerd* (2022) https://moneynerd. co.uk/average-credit-card-debt (accessed 3 August 2022).

Nouwen, Henri. *The Dance of Life: Spiritual Direction with Henri Nouwen*, ed. Michael Ford (London: Darton, Longman & Todd, 2005).

Percey, Andy. *Infused with Life: Exploring God's Gift of Rest in a World of Busyness* (Milton Keynes: Authentic, 2019).

——. *Made to Belong: Moving beyond Tribalism to Find Our True Connection in God* (Milton Keynes: Authentic, 2021).

——. *When Rain Falls Like Lead: Exploring the Presence of God in the Darkness of Suffering* (Milton Keynes: Paternoster, 2013).

Peterson, Eugene. *The Message of David: Earthy Spirituality for Everyday Christians* (London: Marshall Pickering, 1997).

Powell, John. *Why Am I Afraid to Love?* (Chicago, IL: Argus Communications, 1967).

Silk, Danny. *Culture of Honor: Sustaining a Supernatural Environment* (Shippensburg, PA: Destiny Image, 2009).

Stackhouse, Ian. *Praying the Psalms: A Personal Journey through the Psalter* (Eugene, OR: Cascade, 2018).

Westermann, Claus. *Praise and Lament in the Psalms* (Atlanta, GA: John Knox Press, 1981).

Whitfield, Charles L. *The Truth about Depression: Choices for Healing* (Deerfield Beach, FL: Health Communications, 2003).

——. *Wisdom to Know the Difference: Core Issues in Relationships, Recovery and Living* (Atlanta, GA: Muse House Press, 2012).

Wilson, Gerald H. *Psalms, Volume 1*, NIV Application Commentary (Grand Rapids, MI: Zondervan, 2002).

Wolpe, David. *David: The Divided Heart* (London and New Haven, CT: Yale University Press, 2014).

Yancey, Philip. *What's So Amazing about Grace?* (Grand Rapids, MI: Zondervan, 1997).

Made to Belong

*Moving beyond tribalism
to find our true
connection in God*

Andy Percey

Where do I belong?

Since our earliest days, humans have sat around tribal fires and told stories about how we belong. This desire is deeply built into us and the glow of that fire is still enticing.

We long to 'find our tribe' and to fit in with others like us. So, even when we scratch the itch of tribalism, why do we burn for something else? Andy Percey shows us that we were never made to just fit in; God created us to belong to him and each other in the truest and deepest way possible.

If you are asking these questions around the fire, this book is your invitation into relationship, partnership, companionship and belonging.

978-1-78893-185-4

Infused with Life

*Exploring God's gift of rest in
a world of busyness*

Andy Percey

In a stressful, task-orientated life, we know the importance of rest,
but it is too often pushed out of our busy schedules.

Join Andy Percey as he reveals that rest is actually God's good gift to
us, provided for us to experience a balance in our lives that isn't just
about rest as recovery, but rest as harmony with our Creator and the
world he has made.

By learning to practise life-giving rhythms of rest, we can be infused
with the very best of the life God freely gives us.

978-1-78893-065-9

When Rain Falls Like Lead

*Exploring the presence of God
in the darkness of suffering*

Andy Percey

'Why does God allow suffering?' 'Where is God in my suffering?'

These are the big questions that we all grapple with at some point in
our lives. This unique, biblically-rooted and pastorally-focused book
explores these questions in a sensitive and compelling way. Finding
himself wrestling with these questions when his sister died suddenly,
Percey delivers an honest, personal and poignant look at the issues.
Whilst never shying away from the pain and reality of suffering, this
book weaves together biblical truths with genuine hope to help us see
that God really is present, even in the darkness.

978-1-84227-813-0

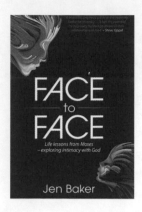

Face to Face

*Life lessons from Moses –
exploring intimacy with God*

Jen Baker

God longs for us to personally experience more of him, but so often we refuse or feel unable to draw close to him. Even the great hero of faith Moses hid his face from God, yet was eventually transformed into someone who spoke face to face with him.

Jen Baker explores Moses' life to see how he was able to move from hiddenness to holiness and encourages us to follow his example. Interwoven with personal testimony, Jen gently challenges and shows us how to move out of the shadows into the light of God's love.

Whether you feel distant from God or want to deepen your relationship with him, *Face to Face* will help encourage you to experience God in a new and powerful way.

978-1-78893-056-7

Finding Our Voice

*Unsung lives from the Bible
resonating with stories from today*

Jeannie Kendall

The Bible is full of stories of people facing issues that are still surprisingly relevant today. Within its pages, people have wrestled with problems such as living with depression, losing a child, overcoming shame, and searching for meaning. Yet these are not always the stories of the well-known heroes of faith, but those of people whose names are not even recorded.

Jeannie Kendall brings these unnamed people to vibrant life. Their experiences are then mirrored by a relevant testimony from someone dealing with a similar situation today.

Finding Our Voice masterfully connects the past with the present day, encouraging us to identify with the characters' stories, and giving us hope that, whatever the circumstances, we are all 'known to God'.

978-1-78893-037-6

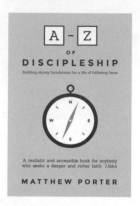

A–Z of Discipleship

Building strong foundations for a life of following Jesus

Matthew Porter

A–Z of Discipleship is an accessible introduction to the understanding and practice of the Christian faith. It presents twenty-six aspects of discipleship to help you grow in your relationship with God, connect with church and live as a follower of Christ in contemporary culture.

Each topic has a few pages of introduction and insight, an action section for reflection and application and a prayer to help put the action point into practice. There are also references to allow further study.

978-1-78078-456-4

30 Days with . . . Emily Owen

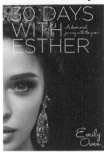

30 Days with Esther
*A devotional journey
with the queen*
978-1-78078-448-9

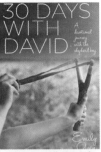

30 Days with David
*A devotional journey
with the shepherd boy*
978-1-78078-449-6

30 Days with Mary
*A devotional journey with
the mother of Jesus*
978-1-86024-935-8

30 Days with Elijah
*A devotional journey
with the prophet*
978-1-86024-937-2

30 Days with Ruth
*A devotional journey
with the loyal widow*
978-1-78893-179-3

30 Days with John
*A devotional journey
with the disciple*
978-1-86024-936-5

Authentic